Pastoral Care and Counseling in Grief and Separation

Creative Pastoral Care and Counseling Series
    Editor: Howard J. Clinebell, Jr.
    Associate Editor: Howard W. Stone

Pastoral Care and Counseling in Grief and Separation

Wayne E. Oates

Fortress Press   Philadelphia

TO
Walter S. Coe, M.D.

Library of Congress Catalog Card Number 75–13048
ISBN 0-8006-0554-3

Third printing 1980

8816J80   Printed in the United States of America   1-554

Contents

Series Foreword

Let me share with you some of the hopes that are in the minds of those of us who helped to develop this series—hopes that relate directly to you as the reader. It is our desire and expectation that these books will be of help to you in developing better working tools as a minister counselor. We hope that they will do this by encouraging your own creativity in developing more effective methods and programs for helping people live life more fully. It is our intention in this series to affirm the many things you have going for you as a minister in helping troubled persons—the many assets and resources from your religious heritage, your role as the leader of a congregation, and your unique relationship to individuals and families throughout the life cycle. We hope to help you reaffirm *the power of the pastoral* by the use of fresh models and methods in your ministry.

The aim of the series is not to be comprehensive with respect to topics but rather to bring innovative approaches to some major types of counseling. Although the books are practice-oriented, they also provide a solid foundation of theological and psychological insights. They are written primarily for ministers (and those preparing for the ministry) but we hope that they will also prove useful to other counselors who are interested in the crucial role of spiritual and value issues in all helping relationships. In addition we hope that the series will be useful in seminary courses, clergy support groups, continuing education workshops, and lay befriender training.

This is a period of rich new developments in counseling and psychotherapy. The time is ripe for a flowering of creative methods and insights in pastoral care and counseling. Our expectation is that this series will stimulate grass roots creativity as innovative methods and programs come alive for you. Some of the major thrusts that will be discussed in this series include a new awareness of the unique contributions of the theologically trained counselor, the liberating power of the human potentials orientation, an appreciation of the pastoral care function of the ministering congregation, the importance of humanizing systems and institutions as well as close relationships, the importance of pastoral *care* (and not just counseling), the many opportunities for caring ministries throughout the life cycle, the deep changes in male-female relationships, and the new psychotherapies such as Gestalt therapy, Transactional Analysis, educative counseling, and crisis methods. Our hope is that this series will enhance your resources for your ministry to persons by opening doorways to understanding of these creative thrusts in pastoral care and counseling.

In this volume, Wayne Oates, one of the pioneers and major contributors to the pastoral care field, presents fresh resources for helping persons experiencing all kinds of losses. He integrates newer methods of helping—from Gestalt therapy, for example—with the wisdom of our religious and pastoral heritage. His own pastoral experience provides the bridge which joins the old and the new. The insights and methods in this book will be useful to anyone—professional or layperson—who deals with the bereaved.

For twenty-six years, Wayne taught pastoral care at the Southern Baptist Seminary in Louisville, Kentucky. During two of those years he was on sabbatical leave and teaching at Union Theological Seminary in New York. Now, he writes from a new job perspective—as Professor of Psychiatry and Behavioral Science at the School of Medicine, University of Louisville, where he teaches both psychiatric and pastoral residents.

The author sees the loss of someone by death as the prototype of other significant losses. He deals in nearly one-fourth of the book with divorce, the death of a relationship. He describes the unique pastoral opportunities in the "killer diseases" and in Elisabeth Kübler-Ross's five stages of dying.* He urges the use of growth groups in ministering to the bereaved, and faces realistically both the limitations and the resources of a pastor in grief caring and counseling. He emphasizes the importance of rituals of community as means of life support during losses, and points to the need for new rituals in losses such as divorce.

One of the strengths of this book is Wayne Oates's sharing of something of his own grief. I found myself moved by his account of his bereavement dream of his grandmother's funeral. In a note to me, he commented that the book was written during a time of double grief. I hope that you'll find that this book speaks to you in your losses and also is helpful in your ministry to other burdened human beings.

HOWARD J. CLINEBELL, JR.

---

* For this and all other notes in this book, see the Notes section beginning on p. 81.

Introduction

The title of this book has been carefully chosen. When I use the term *pastoral care*, I am referring to the total set of resources of church and community that a pastor uses to prevent and to meet grief and separation. When I use the word *counseling* I am referring to the specific instruments of the small group and the individual interviewing process. The pastor and other disciplined counselors aim to make of grief and separation an avenue to constructive growth rather than an occasion for destructive deterioration of the personality. Pastoral counseling, then, is a specific form of intervention on behalf of growth and the achievement of potential; it seeks to oppose the forces of destruction unleashed in the wake of grief and separation.

Furthermore, the title speaks of both *grief* and *separation*. These are overlapping terms: *grief* involves separation from loved objects or persons and *separation* involves grief: both are followed by a process of struggle and growth. However, for the purposes of this small volume, I will use the word *grief* to mean what it means in ordinary everyday parlance: the loss of someone by death. I shall use *separation* to mean the loss of someone or something by a means other than death—by alienation, conflict, accident, or disaster. Probably the most common kind of loss by separation is divorce. But broken courtships, job losses, broken friendships, and losses of homes through financial reverses or natural disasters are also forms of separation that are profoundly akin to the loss of someone by death. Rarely if ever in the popular mind, and only to a certain extent in the technical literature, are the similarities between grief at the loss of someone by death and the grief involved in separation from something or somebody recognized and considered.

The thrust of this book is to relate, without equating, grief and separation. Pastors should come to see the more subtle bereavements of life as clearly as those occasioned by death and to take them as seriously. Even the normal developmental crises of life—such as a child leaving home for the adult tasks of study, marriage, or work—can be appreciated in terms of the separation involved and should be responded to with a subtle seriousness like that extended to persons who have been bereaved by death. The pastor who takes seriously these subtle separations over the years will, in terms of his relationships to people, be better equipped for ministry to the individuals and families who look to him for help in times of terminal illness or death.

The view taken here toward grief and separation is not, therefore, a negative "mournful numbers" approach. Nor is it a "sweet denial" approach that smooths over loss of every kind with easy affirmations that they really are not so. We face head-on the reality of grief and loss. We identify the temptations to unreality that beset the bereaved and estranged person. And we focus on that new life which can be resurrected from the shattering experiences of death and separation —life itself can be affirmed in the decision to live again. The proper approach to grief and separation cannot abide either nostalgia or denial, for it is sacramental in something more than a ritualistic sense of the word.

Pastors find that disciplines of faith turn grief and separation into instruments of fortification and strengthening for other people who are bereaved and estranged. We suffer at times ourselves, but discover that our own afflictions, though never unaccompanied by tears, are freed of whimpering. Indeed, our own afflictions take on added meaning as they bring us new and closer relationships with other people who are hurting. The once agonizing question *why* is dispelled by fascinating discoveries of growth as we share with others who are also in some stage of grief and separation. Our former despairing wonder about *what if* this or that had not happened is supplanted by sheer amazement that inasmuch as this or that has indeed happened I am now empowered to do new things by what I have learned. Once grief and separation are no longer strangers, once we know them for what they are, we find that we can turn and strengthen others who may, by comparison, still be novices at coping with such experiences.

1. Traditional Expectations of the Pastor in Relation to the Bereaved

Through the centuries the pastor has been the primary person responsible for dealing with the bereaved. Traditionally, professional responsibility in relation to death and separation has devolved upon pastor, priest, or rabbi. Whether or not the pastor has accepted these responsibilities, carried them out with skill and wisdom, or even appreciated the weight of the expectations placed upon him or her, nevertheless the pastor is the one to whom people still look for the care of the bereaved, the alienated, and the separated.

For example, in hospitals where a chaplain is a part of the healing team, a subtle shift takes place when a death occurs. The chaplain suddenly becomes the central professional person responsible for the care of the bereaved family after the news of death is brought to them by the physician and/or nurse. Usually the chaplain is asked to be there when the word is passed and the initial hard shock strikes home. People expect much of the pastor; they always have.

The Liability of the Traditional Expectations

Traditional expectations put the chaplain or the pastor in a strategic and often advantageous position for beginning or sustaining a long-term relationship to the family of the deceased. However, this over-identification of the pastor with the care of the bereaved at the time of death can occasionally hinder the pastor's total ministry.

A man I knew called me recently to request help. Fred, a factory worker, asked that I as a minister visit a twenty-three year old housewife in the hospital. Dorothy had just been told that she would have to have her left leg amputated.

4

I asked Fred to go to the hospital with me.   When we arrived, Dorothy's husband Steve was courteous.   Yet he admitted that they were not churchgoing people.   In fact, he added frankly, if I as a strange pastor were to go into the room, his wife might think she was dying.   That was what a pastoral visit meant to Steve—you're dying!

Fred replied: "But Dorothy knows his son, Bill.   *I* will go in with Doctor Oates and introduce him as Bill's daddy.   Then she'll not be afraid.   After she feels comfortable with his being there, I'll remind her—in case she has forgotten—that Doctor Oates is a minister."

Fortunately Dorothy did remember that "Bill's daddy" was also a minister.   She accepted me as such: "I pray, but I'm scared and need your prayers too."

This visit began a longer-term kind of pastoral visitation in which Dorothy was able to confront her situation and face up to her losing a vital limb of her body.   She accepted me as a pastor.   However, if I had not previously had *another* relationship to her—as the father of a person whom she already knew—I may never have been able to get over the obstacle of being thought of as a sort of "death messenger."   The traditional expectation was a hurdle to be scaled.

Dorothy, it should be noted, was not dying, but she was facing separation from a whole limb of her body.   Her reaction to this kind of loss was similar to a grief reaction, as if she were losing a member of her family by death.   Women undergoing a mastectomy and/or hysterectomy, i.e., the surgical removal of a breast and/or uterus, experience major changes in their self-concept, changes which follow the pattern of a grief reaction.   The French proverb, *partir, c'est mourir un peu,* "to part or separate is to die a little," is certainly applicable to the loss of a vital part of the body.

Dorothy's long period of convalescence provided pastoral opportunity for dealing with the process of grief that followed the surgical loss.   Several fears beset her: "How will I look with a false leg?"   "Will my husband lose interest in me and want a different sexual partner?"   "Will I be able to 'be a

wife' to him?" "Will I be able to take care of my little boy?"
Continued counseling brought these and other anxious concerns to the surface. It provided opportunity for guidance
and for enabling her to maintain contact with reality. It was
arranged for her also to be in touch with other amputees who
had "made it" successfully through such an operation, and
these contacts proved important in her coping process. The
pastoral ministry became to her a fellowship of search for new
hope and new directions. As a minister I was no longer a
"death messenger" but a harbinger of hope for the future.

Yet, for better or worse this aura of the "death messenger"
hangs over the pastor. During the Vietnam War, the chaplains near the military bases back home had the grisly task of
"notifying the next of kin" when their men had been killed in
action. Fort Knox is near my home city. I myself assisted in
debriefing chaplains who had participated in these stressful
experiences. In the communities where they appeared in uni-
form they were considered purveyors of "bad news." They
were often met by the local civilians with exceptional and
overt hostility. The pastors had to leap these hurdles, of
course, in order to bring comfort and strength to the people
whose relatives had been killed. Such duty, however, did
much to reenforce the primitive notion that the appearance of
a minister on the scene presages the news of death.

The parish pastor must also confront another primitive
stereotype. In the mind of many people the minister is "not
supposed to know" anything about the angers, the hostilities,
the separations, and the irreconcilable differences that beset
people. There is a common assumption that he or she knows
nothing of this, and a corresponding taboo against the minister ever mentioning it. Direct, forthright, and candid personal
expression causes people to withdraw in astonished silence. If
the pastor ever becomes angry or shows a burst of temper, he
or she is censored. Therefore, people tend to keep a minister
carefully ignorant of their own hostile and inflamed relationships. These denials of anger and alienation often continue
until the deep differences are disclosed by some overt action

reported in the newspaper. Too often the pastor is "the last to know." By the time the minister does become knowledge-able about the conflicts, they are "past the point of no return."

Examples of this abound. A businessman is indicted for fraudulent and illegal business practices. Members of his own congregation—other businessmen, accountants, lawyers, and secretaries—"knew all about it." Yet every attempt is made to keep the pastor unaware of the impending tragedy until the whole story is publicly revealed.

Probably the most common of all the problems cloaked in such a veil of secrecy by a congregation is that of marital alienation, separation, and divorce. The pastor of a church often learns of a marital conflict only in its later stages when separation, legal action, or divorce finally brings it to his or her attention. One of the major reasons for this blackout of communication is the traditional projection of the "illusion of respectability" upon the minister. Then too, taboos upon divorce are often maintained by pastors. The commitment of the church to the durability of marriage, and the dubious as-sumption that infidelity is the likely cause of divorce, together conspire to exclude the pastor from such separating experi-ences in people's lives. The traditional ministerial stance that reconciliation is the *only* viable alternative prompts the couple to assume that the minister will not "listen to" any other op-tion, not even that of temporary separation. As a result, cou-ples in conflict often will not come to the pastor at all.

Such taboos pose ethical dilemmas for pastors: Do we as pastors engage only in marriage counseling? Or, do we also do divorce counseling? Divorce counseling does not neces-sarily mean that we *advise* divorce. It does mean that we face the reality of divorce as *one* of the options that people increas-ingly choose in dealing with marital conflict. Our options are to face with them the reality of divorce—as a possibility, not a necessity—*or* refer them to lawyers, not just for legal advice but for the total counseling process. The latter option is likely to separate the couple not only from each other but also from continuing pastoral care.

The pastor may choose yet another option, however: he may continue pastoral counseling of the couple even while they are in the process of consulting a lawyer and getting a divorce. Even when pastors attempt this, however, post-divorce counseling is often broken off anyway by one or both parties.

The kinds of bereavement experienced within and between individuals securing a divorce are intense, especially where children are involved. The infections and complications of the bereavement process, however, are not absolutely necessary and foreordained. On the contrary, new vistas of growth and learning can be opened if the hardness of heart often associated with divorce can be reduced or transcended in and through the attendant suffering. In any given instance, however, the pastor will have to scale the hurdle of the traditional stereotype that all pastors are deaf to anything but the total "kiss-and-make-up" approach to marriage counseling.

Challenging the Traditional Expectations

When people discover they can grow through loss, and that pastors can facilitate that growth, can help them reduce isolation and loneliness and begin to interpret the shape of things to come, they revise their stereotypes. The pastoral encounter comes to be seen as "good news" rather than "bad news." If the resurrected life means anything at all it means good news in the face of grief and separation:

> For I am sure that neither death, nor life, nor angels, nor principalities, nor things present, nor things to come, nor powers, nor height, nor depth, nor anything else in all creation, will be able to separate us from the love of God in Christ Jesus our Lord.
>
> —Romans 8:38–39

In the name of this "pastoral persuasion" it is essential to confront the hindrances and barriers to pastoral care and counseling in grief and separation. The alert and innovative pastor will seek to develop a strategy and a set of tactical procedures for gaining entrée early into the processes of grief and separation.   The remainder of this book aims at helping the pastoral counselor do just that.   Special attention will be given to three areas of special concern to pastors and spiritual counselors.

First, considerable research and attention has gone into identifying the dynamic processes involved in grief and separation.   Knowing these processes enables the pastor to develop a "distant early warning" detection system, and to discover "clues" into the real needs of people often before they have themselves detected their own need.

Inherent in the processes of grief and separation are patterns of blaming and self-condemnation, the attributing of responsibility to others and to oneself.   Gestalt psychology calls these patterns "projections" and "introjections."*   In both cases the responsibility is unevenly distributed.   Considerable confusion attends the processes of grief and separation; things tend to flow together and become blurred.   Human vision normally affords an analogy: we keep a fairly clear view of those things on which we focus our attention at any given time; however, confusion occurs in the field of our peripheral vision.   Similarly, our subjective feelings of grief and separation tend usually to be more like peripheral than focal vision —confused.   For this reason, in addition to the faulty distribution of responsibility associated with projections and introjections, Gestalt psychologists speak of "confluence," things flowing together.†   Consequently the process of grief and separation may not be regarded as involving an easily timed step-by-step procession of developmental stages, always distinct, sequential, and easily identifiable.   In any given instance the stages of reaction flow together in confusion from time to time.

The pastor can, through observation, sense and learn to identify these various stages and processes.   The projections in grief and separation, for example, are best identified in the *why* conversations of people, the introjections in their *if* conversations.   The confluences tend to push the person into closer touch with or greater detachment from reality.   Awareness of these dynamics provides the pastor with indices of growth and calls for tactics that will avoid arresting the processes of growth. We will trace these processes.

Second, the pastor as a community person has access to already established rituals such as weddings, funerals, christenings, baptisms, pastoral visitation, and natural group formations with which to intervene in the processes of grief and separation. Additionally, the innovative pastor can also learn new rituals for intervention from some of the newer human potential techniques. Some of these will be suggested in due course as we explore in detail the processes of grief and separation. Rituals both old and new can contribute to growth, freedom, and the expansion of awareness and human potential.

Third, the pastor is at best a practical mystic in touch with powerful belief systems and with the powers of blessing and cursing in the universe. The charismatic strength of the pastor working in relation to the God and Father of our Lord Jesus Christ cannot be mundanely discounted simply because of popular distortions of the meaning of charisma. On the contrary, the power of the pastor's being points to the Presence of God. Even out of the depths of silence itself, nonverbal communication of that power can come from the pastor individually, or in the company where two or three are gathered together in the name of Christ. It will be our purpose also to explore this theme, namely, the relation of persuasion to the calling forth of the bereaved from nostalgia to adventure in new growth.

2. Anticipatory Grief and Separation

Intelligent anticipation of events before they occur is a distinctive and vital function of the human person. Separating fact from fantasy, however, and keeping fantasied anticipation from *causing* itself to become a fact, is an even more exquisite ability and responsibility of the human person. Sometimes we run when no one pursues. Occasionally we even continue running when intellectually we *know* that no one is pursuing. These mysterious capacities of the human person are what enable and prompt us to be apprehensive at the possibility of separation or death.

Apprehension has a double meaning. It means to lay hold of, catch, capture or understand something; it also means to feel threatened, fearful, or anxious about what might happen. Apprehensiveness as the darker, more pessimistic side of anticipation is what we want to consider in relation to grief and separation.

Plainly, grief and separation are dealt with pastorally in two markedly different ways, depending upon how they begin. There are two kinds of onset: the slow, insidious, and prolonged onset, and the acute, sudden, and cataclysmic onset. One kind of dealing is appropriate with the family who has lost someone after a long, delaying-action battle with terminal disease, another with the person who, after enjoying a happy evening meal, pleasant conversation, and a good night's rest awakens to discover a dead spouse lying in the same bed— victim of a heart attack. Similarly, divergent care is indicated when a divorce occurs suddenly, without warning, and when the divorce represents the obvious culmination of a long, tortuous period of conflict and infighting. In this chapter, we will deal with the first kind of situation, the anticipated grief and separation. In the next chapter we will deal with the sudden and unexpected variety.

Anticipating Death

"Anticipatory grief," according to the noted author on grief, Erich Lindemann, designates the process in which a bereaved person "goes through all the phases of grief" in advance, as a safeguard against the impact expected when the death notification occurs.* Such grief can mean nothing more than a disastrous conditioning effect if the patient should dramatically recover instead of dying, as for example when a supposedly terminal illness proves to have been wrongly diagnosed. Acute and sudden grief has by contrast, an awful finality about it. Anticipatory grief involves the "weight of waiting," the indeterminateness that mingles a sense of relief with the sense of loss when death finally comes. Pastors need to alert the family in advance to the fact that this sense of relief should not be accompanied with guilt feelings but with gratitude.

The Processes of Anticipation

Elisabeth Kübler-Ross has described the process of experientially becoming attuned to the reality of one's own death as one deals with dying patients.† In terms of Gestalt psychology, the principle involved is that of "congruence."‡ Death is ordinarily seen, felt, and spoken about as something alien to and out of tune with life. Discovering some connection and/or compatibility between life and death is a process. Learning to live with death as a reality is an achievement. The process—and the achievement—is both physical and psychic.

Wolfgang Kohler states the principle of congruence by saying that "all experienced order in space" *at the level of awareness* finds some "corresponding order in the underlying dynamic context of physiological processes."§ As bodily changes occur, states of consciousness associated with these changes simultaneously occur. Yet, at the unconscious level, we develop projections, introjections, confluences, and "retro-flections" which fracture or segment this connection and/or compatibility—congruence—of consciousness with physiological processes.* Perls, Hefferline, and Goodman put it this way:

> A man is ill; he tries to go about his business and he suffers; forced to realize he has quite other business, he attends to his illness, lies down and waits; the suffering lessens and he falls asleep. Or, a loved one dies; there is a sad conflict between intellectual acceptance on the one hand and desires and memories on the other. The average man tries to distract himself, but the superior man obeys the signal and engages himself in the suffering, calls up the past, sees his present hopelessly frustrated; he cannot imagine what to do now that his bottom has fallen out of everything; the grief, and suffering are prolonged, for there is much to be destroyed and annihilated and much to be assimilated, and during this time, he must not go about his unimportant business deliberately suppressing the conflict. Finally, the mourning's labor is complete and the person is changed, he assumes a creative disinterest; at once new interests become dominant.†

The internal conflict and struggle connected with death and dying can be dangerous. Perls, Hefferline, and Goodman continue: "Mourning as a means of letting go the old self to change explains why mourning is attended by self-destructive behavior like scratching the skin, beating the breast, tearing the hair."‡ The person may tear himself to pieces with anger, guilt, and resistance to reality. The goal of pastoral care and counseling, though, is not to weaken the conflict but to strengthen the self and self-awareness so that the self may grow in the real world as it is. Thus the suffering connected with grief and separation may produce a measure of growth not easily experienced in any other way.

Stages of Awareness in Dying

The work of Elisabeth Kübler-Ross identifies stages in the process of growth in the awareness and acceptance of the reality of death in dying patients.§ The incongruity between the life and death *can* be overcome. For the dying, physiological death can be experienced as a part of life; dying and grief are inseparable but not the same. For the mourning loved ones too, the incongruity between past security and present pain can be overcome; there is a future for one's independent selfhood apart from the deceased. For both the dying and the bereaved, the congruent life is a possibility.

Kübler-Ross's work deals more with the anticipatory kind of grief than with acute grief in that her research is primarily with terminally ill persons as they move from one stage of physiological deterioration to another. The process of anticipatory grief goes on also in the family as they stand by and see their beloved separated from one vital bodily function after another. Kübler-Ross identifies five stages in the process of awareness-change in the dying patient. In columns parallel to the one detailing her five stages of patient reaction, I have tried on pp. 16–17 to list the corresponding changes in family reaction, medical intervention, and pastoral intervention. The counselor needs to be aware of all of them simultaneously.

Kübler-Ross's descriptions of the five phases of anticipatory grief do not purport to be neat categories each of which ends precisely where the next appears. On the contrary, temporary remission of symptoms, the permission to use experimental treatments, or other factors can all complicate the process to the point where the five stages overlap or are confused with one another. Feelings are not respecters of categories. Even the ancients were aware of the dynamic flux and confluence of many emotions: the various biblical words normally translated "to grieve" at root really mean "to be angry," "to be weary," "to feel disgusted," "to be bitter," "to be pained," "to be solicitous."

The pattern outlined by Kübler-Ross helps us, however, to deal with the confusion of emotions, which at times can result in a loss of touch with reality. Perls says that "confluence is a condition of no-contact (no self boundary). This is 'getting out of touch' and becoming a stranger even to oneself. Even so, important interacting is going on, for instance physiological functioning, environmental stimulation, etc."* The terminally ill patient, at least potentially, is quite capable of contacting the nature of his/her physiological functioning and of contacting the "significant others" around. The pastor is—or, hopefully can become—one of those "significant others." Where the patient clings to unawareness, he/she achieves security without satisfaction; nothing new occurs, and interest in the old is lost.

Creating Awareness

The awareness-creating approaches available to a pastor for anticipatory grief and separation are many. Let me suggest just four:

Data collection and apprehension slowdown. The intelligent anticipation of events before they occur does not happen in a data-less, fact-less void. It is a trigonometric process. The careful assessment of two points on a map provides a third point on the same map. Early signs of cancer, tuberculosis, and heart disorder can be put together to suggest that the pastor urge a person to seek medical diagnosis. Heightened anxiety can be slowed down by urging a "wait-and-see" attitude. A thorough diagnosis has therapeutic value; it removes some of the fear engendered by the unknown and by hasty self-diagnoses filled with "my theological" constructs as to what is or is not "going on" in one's own physiology. The pastor needs to be *aware* of his/her own body and to listen carefully to such realities as pain, fatigue, hyperactivity, and rigidity in the bodies of the counselees.

The American Cancer Society is actively engaged in organizing groups of identifiable cancer patients who do a great deal of "data collection and apprehension slowdown" together. They get in touch with professionals for data and stay in touch with each other and with professional counselors by telephone. The main function of such data collection and apprehension slowdown is to become aware of one's own body —its strengths as well as its limitations.

Getting in touch with anger. Anger is a natural response to injustice. A pastor can facilitate the anticipatory grief by

PATIENT REACTION	FAMILY REACTION
1. *Denial.* Disbelief. Isolation. The decision to share or not to share his/her feelings.	Shifting roles. Quest for a support community. Need for "stress-breaks." Decisions whether or not to communicate such facts as are known. How to "break the wall of silence."
2. *Anger.* Finding adequate targets for anger. God is most adequate. Catharsis.	Sharing of anger as injustice, without taking too personally or patronizingly the anger of the loved one directed at them.
3. *Bargaining.* Review of past infidelities to man and God. Reversion to the image of self as a "lucky" or "unlucky" person.	Review of past conflicts in the light of the new situation. Renewal of marriage vows, for example. Repentance for overwork and neglect.
4. *Despair.* Depression. Mourning at the loss of parts of body, changes in appearance, disability. Despair over excessive costs of care. Loss of job.	Avoidance of cheerleader role. Frank weeping with the weeping patient. Assurance of loving steadfastness. Avoidance of suspicion of marital unfaithfulness.
5. *Acceptance.* Extending the amount of sleep—exactly the reverse of decreasing it as with a child. "A final rest before a long journey." "I have fought all I can."	Restricting visits only to persons intimately known by or asked for by the patient. Being with the patient and keeping alert for leave-taking messages, verbal and nonverbal. Elimination of all family infighting.

MEDICAL INTERVENTION	PASTORAL INTERVENTION
Physician's certainty of diagnosis. Need for consultation. Sustaining interest in a dying patient; combating boredom. Establishing an open relationship with family and patient. Helplessness. "Busyness."	Awareness of the patient's shock and need for denial. Debriefing after diagnosis. Encouragement of medical consultation. Reenforcement of health maintenance presumptions.
Absorbing anger directed at him/her and carefully protecting the patient's needless running from doctor to doctor by suggesting consultations.	Creation of an "OK" feeling about anger, especially toward God.
Could money buy better treatment? Could it all be psychological? Should a psychiatrist be called in?	Rededications to God. Vows to enter religious work. Vows to attend church more. Let's live each day at a time.
Possible use of medication to control anxiety and/or depression.	Encouraging the expression of sorrow. Avoiding over-reassurance. Sitting with the person in silence. Touch. Prayer.
Being sure that the patient is not forgotten. Being alone with the patient at eventide. Close consultation with the family about the use of artificial means to extend life.	Regular visiting according to previous patterns. Listening for confessions—good and bad. Listening for last requests, funeral wishes, estate planning. "Nothing can separate us."

exploring with an individual or group of persons what they consider to be the greatest injustice they have suffered. In one such group, Joe was evidently in great fear of impending disability and death. He dealt with the question directly and sharply: "God brought this terrible pain upon me when I was at the very peak of my productive work. I think that is the greatest injustice I have ever suffered!" For Joe it was much easier to get in touch with his feelings of injustice through blaming God than to accept himself as being a very angry person—something that was abhorrent to him at that time. Among religious peoples particularly, the word *anger* is often a taboo word, a "signal reaction" that provokes negative emotions and blocks clear perception. It was not until weeks later that Joe could acknowledge personal responsibility for his own anger, and then he spoke of himself as being stubborn! Muriel James and Dorothy Jongeward suggest that the following directions can be either taken personally or given to a group for getting in touch with anger:

> Become aware of your body's response to your anger. Do you restrict or hold back some part of your body? Clench your teeth? Fist? Colon? Exaggerate your restriction. What do you discover?*

The person who is in the stage of anger in anticipating grief may also focus this anger on some*one*. In conversation with a pastor or a group the angry person might name this other person out loud and find a phrase that fits his or her own feeling: "Stop trying to baby me." "Stop trying to tell me how I feel." "Stop protecting me." "Stop changing the subject when I mention dying."

Anticipating depression. A pastor can effectively anticipate times of depression in persons with terminal illness. Certain kinds of treatment such as cobalt therapy are themselves demanding. They are apt to prove exhausting, and exhaustion is often mingled with depression. Blaming of self or others again goes hand in hand with depression. Self-depreciation can take the form of the patient or the family member accepting *total* responsibility for the disaster of impending death. Alternately, the person may project blame entirely upon the physician, the driver of the other car, or whoever else around affords a convenient scapegoat. These introjections and projections of responsibility are perfectly normal and can be worked through; guilt and anger can be redistributed until each of the principals bears an appropriately proportioned load. The principle of pastoral care and counseling here is the even or realistic distribution of responsibility.

Death education. Ideally, the pastoral care of persons facing death—and that includes all persons—would include "death education" in the overall spiritual instruction of the whole congregation. Death and dying would then have been faced long before a specific individual or family encounters them existentially. In a group focusing on that theme pastors can use written exercises as a "springboard" for opening up the conversation. Discussion can produce a feeling of acquaintance if not intimacy with death.*

For such death groups, James and Jongeward suggest the use of fantasy-explanations.† A fantasy-explanation takes seriously things we all think about privately and consider too silly or anxiety-provoking to talk about with others. The group is invited to bring forth their fantasies on the theme in such a way as to facilitate the kind of open discussion which can validate and affirm the private thoughts of group members. Individuals may be surprised to discover that others have often had similar if not identical thoughts. Personal notions once privately suspect as strange can be tested by the reality of a common human experience, and mutual support can be developed.

Death education, the formal or informal imparting of knowledge and experience about death and dying, has become a vital force in both the technical literature and the popular press today. Classical literature dealing with death has often served as a foil for private and group reflection on the subject, enabling people to discuss the matter without becoming too personal about it. James Agee's *A Death in the Family* reflects the reality and fantasy struggle of a child with the death of a parent.* Leo Tolstoy's *The Death of Ivan Illyich* describes in progressive detail the inner reactions of an adult who is facing gradually the impending reality of his own death.† In *A Grief Observed* C. S. Lewis comes more nearly to being autobiographical and telling in detail his own experience at the loss of his wife.‡ Betty Bryant, using excerpts from her journal, shares the emotional and spiritual odyssey of her first six months of widowhood in *Leaning Into the Wind: The Wilderness of Widowhood.*§

Today, the scientific community, which includes a significant number of the parish pastors of the country in the clinical pastoral education movement, has begun to develop empirical models for the conduct of existential "here-and-now" growth groups dealing with death. These groups seek to deal with both dream and reality in the confrontation of one's own dying and of the death of significant loved ones.

Concluding Observations

My own bedside ministry to patients and their families at times of anticipated or imminent death has taught me several things, brought me to several "conclusions," worth summarizing. I state them as the observations of one who knows in part and prophesies in part, but these could well become hypotheses for clinical pastoral research.

First, medical diagnoses of leukemia or cancer or other terminal illnesses have proved to be wrong just often enough to warrant at least thorough consultation with more than one physician, and a guarded encouragement of a "wait-and-see" attitude such as, "Let's live each day fully as though it were our last. This *could* be *my* last day of life in the kind of world of chance and circumstance in which I live. I will join you in living this way."

Second, medical knowledge about the symptoms and treatment of "killer" diseases has been spread widely enough on television, radio, and in written form for the average patient to know far more about his or her own state of health than the family, the doctor, or the minister may assume. I have found that the *patient* usually tells *me*—if I have the patience for unhurried listening, if I am not panicked by the very mention of death, and if I join the patient in facing both life and death in their interrelatedness.

Third, medical knowledge of killer diseases is so widely disseminated that a few people live in inordinate fear of terminal illness. They have been so programmed by others, or their anxiety is sufficiently high, that the phobia of one of these killer diseases becomes a controlling factor in their lives. In a psychiatric hospital such patients are not at all uncommon. The phenomenon occurs often enough to justify the assertion that culture *can* program anxieties into pseudodiagnoses. The death *wish* is often powerful enough to actualize the thing wished for. Suicidal intentions take some bizarre forms at times. Why does this person seem to need to die? My own strategy is always to push for a thorough diagnosis, which, in these cases may, upon a physician's recommendation, include psychiatric consultation.

Fourth, the body itself has a counselor's wisdom of its own. The vital processes of pain, respiration, heart action, and psychological awareness mysteriously collaborate together to facilitate the five-stage process of reaction to imminent death which Kübler-Ross has described. I am not informed enough nor wise enough to say *how* this happens, but I am mystically inclined enough to cooperate with this "wisdom of the body," to use Walter B. Cannon's words.*

Finally, the will and intention to live is operative in the outcome of some of the most potentially disastrous illnesses. It has sometimes been said that a person is immortal until his or her work is done. I have seen mothers of grown daughters seemingly "wait" until after the wedding of their daughter before they die. I saw one man in his eighties survive four serious heart attacks. He felt that God intended that he should live to "take care" of his wife until *she* died. Ten days after her death, he told the pastor his work was done, he was ready to go now; and he died quietly in his sleep that night. A physician with whom I worked once said: "There is a moving point in the prognosis of many patients' illnesses in which the simple will to live, the reason for being, makes the differences between life and death." The other side of this same coin may be reflected in the death of some patients who have no clinically urgent signs of imminent death. As folk wisdom puts it, some lonely or unhappy people seem simply to "lie down and die." The focii of this mystery are as many as the mystery surrounding the reasons some physiologically capable couples never have children. Both matters need careful clinical pastoral research.

Anticipatory grief in the face of the impending death of a loved family member is vividly expressed in the words of a widow who wrote to me after reading a chapter on the anxiety of grief in my book *Anxiety in Christian Experience.**

> Your chapter on *Grief* interested me very much. I don't believe that I have ever read an analysis of the processes of grief before, or if I did, it did not register because I had not experienced it. All the elements you mentioned have been contained in my own experience, yet for the most part they came before Ivan's death instead of after, undoubtedly because I had known for so long, and had believed what the doctors had told me concerning the nature of Ivan's illness. There has been despair and guilt, but the guilt has been at a minimum—not that I have felt myself worthy or superior, but that I could see, quite clearly I think, that Ivan's trouble was nothing that either he or I could have in any way caused. Rather it was a "chance" of nature, the risk that any one of us takes because we have a physical body and live in this complicated material world. It is something we all must accept, and in one sense be prepared for, to be mature enough to realize that the rain falls on the just and unjust alike.

Separation in Marriage and Divorce

A marriage begins with vast vistas of separateness between the two persons regardless of how "alike" or "together" they may feel. Much counseling literature has been tacitly based upon the myth that marriages are built on *similarities* in age, religion, education, social class, interests, and vocational commitment. More recent emphases, however, have begun to point toward a couple's having to learn *from each other* concerning their *differences*.

The basic difference, of course, more fundamental than the varied backgrounds and skills of the two persons, is the fact that one is a man and the other a woman, with all that that implies in any given society. The experience of "otherness" or "difference" can subtly and often quickly degenerate into "betterness" and "worseness," superiority and inferiority, if role stereotypes keep the man and the woman from understanding each other as persons rather than just as objects fulfilling certain sexual functions or social beings conforming to specified societal patterns.

Maleness/femaleness is not the only difference, however. One spouse may have been brought up in the kind of a family where each member helps the other through "thick and thin." The other spouse may have been brought up in an entirely different setting in which each individual fended for himself or herself, where to receive help, especially from one's parental family, was a sign of weakness and dependence. There may be a difference in attitudes toward work and play. Courtship can be an illusory relationship if it is built around play, parties, and the rituals of leisure time. Marriage by contrast seems harsh because it is built around work, production, maintenance, and economics.

These are just a few of the "separatenesses" a man and a woman bring to marriage. The experience of otherness normally means collision and conflict. In the face of this quite ordinary experience the partners really have three options: to learn from each other's differentness and begin to incorporate the differences into their own being as loved attributes of the other—thus the "two become one"; to "let each other be," which at best can mean only respecting the other's individuality while maintaining one's own uniqueness—no incorporating of another's attributes into oneself; or to reject the other and neither learn from nor respect the partner's differentness —this is "hardness of heart" or unwillingness to learn.

In the presence of this third alternative, separateness and uniqueness harden into patterns of, separation, isolation, and the feeling of being misunderstood and rejected. Acceptance of partners *as they are* seems to be the soil, the water, and the nutrition out of which growth and change take place. Rejection of the other's uniqueness is the stuff out of which separation grows. And as it grows, separation moves through a process similar to that of anticipatory grief. One can again almost chart the course of the development.

Stages in Separation

Stage 1: Unilateral decision making. Decisions are a part of everyday life in every home. Whether these decisions concern work, money, sex, social activities, or the care of children, they almost always involve the scheduling of time, the utilization of leisure, the investment of energy, or the use of money. Decisions that could be the occasion for discussion and contact come to be made individually instead, without mutual consultation.

Stage 2: Mutual deception. From a religious point of view, human relationships are based on open covenants openly arrived at and faithfully kept. When spouses begin to deceive one another the resultant gamesmanship leads to the use of distance-making gambits. Indeed, the very purpose of a "game," in the parlance of Transactional Analysis, is to *create* separation or distance on the basis of covertness and cleverness.* These games are at least a threat to the marriage covenant and at most a deadly assault upon it. The element of trust is the most important ingredient of love, and when deliberate lying takes place—for whatever reason—the developing separation is far along the way toward the point of no return.

Stage 3: Withdrawal into despair. When husband and wife "give up" on each other, each experiences a sense of hopelessness and despair. There is the feeling of being "trapped." The resultant stress may find expression in various addictions, the most common of which are overwork, overeating, overdrinking, and the overuse of drugs. Or, it may lead to some kind of physical illness, the most common of which seem to be generalized gastro-intestinal disorders, upper respiratory problems, and disorders of the genito-urinary system, even including sexual impotence and/or frigidity.

Usually when separation has gotten this far along sexual relationship has either ceased or is very rare. The rituals of attachment—locating, tracking with one's eyes and ears, reaching out to, touching, holding, caressing—have been replaced by an almost opposite set of rituals—not knowing where the other is, withdrawing from bodily contact, pushing the other away, striking in rage, avoiding the sight and sound of the other. In public, these signs of separation can be noted even by strangers, but especially by an observant pastor.

While the symptoms connected with stages one and two may go largely undetected by the pastor, his notice of those involved in stage three immediately raises the question of pastoral intervention. The pastor has a variety of places for contact and tools of ministry at his disposal. He can call by phone, or visit the home, or office, or shopping center at a strategic moment. A pastor can intervene directly: "I wondered if you were feeling well and happy . . ." More difficult than the *how* of intervention is that concerning its degree and quality.* I suggest the utmost of tact in intervention at this stage of separation because both parties to the marriage are presently anxious about whether other people are aware of their unhappiness; they are wondering to whom they can turn for conversation, understanding, and sympathy. Occasionally their concern is mixed with a desire for guidance and counseling. In short, they are on the verge of involving other people in their plight.

Stage 4: Social involvement. Eventually the burdens and stresses are such that the principals tend to involve others in their plight. These may be a third party in an extramarital affair, close friends of the same sex, relatives, and professional counselors—not infrequently in that order. Other unhappy couples and divorced people tend to "sense" quickly who is hurting from intensifying marital separation. Watchful parents seem constantly to be aware of how happy or unhappy their married sons and daughters are. Siblings confide in each

other. Every day physicians see patients whose physical ail-
ments are directly related to their marriage problems; they
bring to the doctor various sexual dysfunctions, psychophysiological disorders, alcoholic syndromes, problems of sterility,
questions about how to have either fewer children or no children at all. In one way or another family conflict repeatedly
comes to a physician's attention.* In many instances, particularly where their own parishioners are concerned, pastors
will be sought out for help and counsel.

The professional person, however, tends *not* to be the first
"outsider" to be involved in marital separation. Close friends
tend to be first. Many times close friends are empathic,
nonpossessively warm, and genuine. Endowed with gener-
ous measure of human wisdom, they can often be bridges
over the troubled waters of separation. If, however, they
have a need of their own that can be met by seeing the chasm
widened, they are driven by forces within to widen the breach
they are called upon to heal. A person of the same sex can,
for example, be prejudiced against the opposite sex in general
with a sort of "settled aversion," or looking for erotic gratifica-
tion of a latent or overt homosexual nature. A person of the
opposite sex may be more interested in having an "affair" with
the confidante friend.

The greatest hazards of an extramarital affair are not primarily to the deteriorating marriage—although an affair generally aids and abets a separation process that otherwise might
be reversible—but to any new marriage that could eventuate
from the affair. There is, first of all, the danger of choosing a
partner who on the surface seems to be altogether different
from the spouse one is leaving but is essentially quite similar in
personality makeup. Second, there is the hazard of entering a
new relationship without having worked through and com-
pleted the grief process involved in the separation and divorce.
My own feeling is that a person should wait at least a year
after the legal termination of divorce proceedings before *starting* another set of marriage intentions, and these should preferably be with someone not intimately involved in the process

of separation and divorce. Third, there is the hazard of distrust built into the new marriage from the outset; if the marital partner deceived his or her spouse in order to form a liaison with someone else, that someone else—who knows of the deception and cooperates in it—may well be infected with suspicion later on.

I am aware that more recent adventures in new lifestyles for both married and unmarried persons provide for more open relationships to people of the opposite sex. Yet the weight of the older mores still affects even the most sophisticated of our contemporaries. Hence, I would underscore the importance of nonpossessiveness, not only in marital partners but also in friends who might be eager to "help" in the distress of separation and/or impending divorce. Also, once a couple gets into the process of separation—even a couple that has never been formally married—the process is likely to follow closely the course I have described thus far. I say this on the basis of a limited number of counselees whom I have served who are "living together" but are not legally married. These couples too tend to revert to the older cultural script about "sneaking around," playing marriage deception games with each other.

Pastoral care and counseling at the stage of social involvement calls for two important procedures: the pastor should learn through direct questioning to whom else the spouses have talked, and he should ask what kinds of advice and counsel they have received, what kinds of promises and agreements they have made with others, both individually and as a couple. Usually this is best done in separate interviews with each spouse rather than with both of them together.

Stage 5: Physical and social separation. By this time much subtle "in-house" separation has gone on. The rituals of attachment have long since ceased. The couple are known by their friends and relatives to be "having trouble" with each other. Now, the separation becomes more obvious and formal when they cease to live in the same apartment or house. This separation—from "bed and board" as legal parlance puts it—can happen in at least a couple different ways.

First, there is what might be called the chaotic separation in which one or the other moves out in the middle of a raging argument or quarrel. Impulsive separations of this sort tend to be short-lived. Tempers cool and spouses often come back together again. Indeed, this kind of "see-saw" action—out again in again—may occur repeatedly.

The planned separation or therapeutic separation, on the contrary, may be undertaken as a deliberate and joint attempt to regain perspective and to prevent further mutual hurt. A pastoral counselor can suggest such a planned separation as a wise and effective way to test a couple's threats of divorce: "If you have already decided to get a divorce, I believe I can be of real service to you as you carry through with your plans, for both of you will need a pastor. However, I would suggest that before you resort to legal steps in dissolving your marriage you try out your decision in an agreed upon, planned separation." Of course, such a test period should be accompanied throughout by individual counseling of both parties. I have seen this "disengagement period" effectively change spouses' attitudes toward each other. I have seen a few couples reconstitute their marriage and renegotiate their expectations of each other. In other instances, I have seen such a planned separation "smoke out" hidden agendas, such as a mistress or paramour relationship or both. In any event, the couple knows in the end that they gave their marriage every opportunity to survive before they finally broke it up.

Such separations can be planned on a legal basis. In many states, separation from eating and sleeping together for specified lengths of time is sufficient "grounds" for divorce. A lawyer can draw up separation papers which establish this fact legally with the passage of time.

From a biblical point of view, a separation "by agreement for a season" in order that a couple may give themselves to prayer as individuals before God is recommended by the Apostle Paul in 1 Corinthians 7:5. Each spouse has his/her own individual relationship to God that needs renewing. Marriage is a finite, human institution; in the resurrection,

Jesus said, there is to be neither marriage nor giving in marriage. The compulsive panic that goes with much marital conflict amounts to idolatry of the institution itself and of the marital partner. Separation for the purpose of prayer can serve the religious necessity of keeping ourselves from idols.

It can also teach us to accept the other's frailties, and to keep our own frailties in focus as well. Such times of separation should be for short periods only. Otherwise, the intended prayer and meditation are supplanted by more tawdry goals. The time can be used to encourage self-examination. A spouse can say about himself or herself all the negative things he or she has thought about his or her mate. Much projection of responsibility goes on in marital conflict; the very atmosphere seems paranoid. During the planned separation such projections can be tested.

"Homework" can be assigned in which one person writes down all the faults of the other:

> "She never listens to anything I say."
> "He just won't do anything I ask him to do."

These same indictments can then be rewritten in the first person singular:

> "*I* never listen to anything she says."
> "*I* just won't do anything he asks me to do."

Additional assignments can also be made. Patterns of self-blame can be written down.

> "If only I were able to earn more money I could make her happy."
> "If only I had a better house and we had more privacy, I could make him happy."

These too can be reversed by saying instead:

> "Does she really expect me to make more money to make her happy?"
> "Does he really want another house, and is privacy as important to him as it is to me?"

Reinterpreting one's own projections is a way of learning from the other. And this is the crucial issue in a separation pending a divorce: do the persons involved have the capacity to learn from each other, to open the self to what is different, other, and dissimilar in the other? As Jesus put it, teachableness is the heart of marriage: unteachableness is the core of divorce: "He answered, 'It was because you were so unteachable that Moses gave you permission to divorce your wives; but it was not like that when all began' " (Matt. 19:8 NEB).

Such teachableness opens the way to renegotiating a marriage relationship. Many couples, often after years of marriage, suddenly awaken one day to realize that essentially they are strangers to each other. This throws them into panic and they begin to make major errors of judgment and behavior in relation to each other. In their panic, they do not take the time to change their pace and priorities long enough to meet each other anew and become reacquainted with each other.

Marriage enrichment groups can often aid couples in getting acquainted with one another as husbands and wives.* Such groups can sometimes facilitate a reacquaintance of separated and estranged couples. Pastors are natural leaders or facilitators of such groups. No procedure, though, is guaranteed to accomplish such an end. If hardness of heart commanded the respect of Moses and Jesus, it should at least give us pause to question any quick judgment that we ourselves are failures as counselors when the marriage moves into the further phases of dissolution.

Stage 6: Legal divorce. When a couple asks the pastor to be a "judge and divider" over them, they are manifestly seeking legal aid, not pastoral care and counseling. "Do you think we should divide the property this way or that?" "Who do you think should keep the children?" "Is he legally bound to support the children?" "I have left him, how can I make him leave me alone?" When questions such as these come to the fore referral is indicated. The pastor can ask if a lawyer has been consulted, perhaps even help to find one.

The relationship between husband and wife at this stage regresses to that of a sibling rivalry. The pastor may be expected by the spouses to provide information about or even against each other. Such manipulation should be resisted. It is my observation that at this stage, one or the other spouse—but not both—will stay in touch with the pastor. For me, at least, it has rarely been possible to maintain contact with both, and the one who does stay in touch often does so only as a way of "keeping up with" and "finding out about" the activities of the other. When this purpose is not served, even that one partner loses interest and tends to fade away.

When a divorce decree has been granted, someone has to take the initiative in keeping the couple, now divorcées, involved. Often a parent with children to raise will double his or her devotion to the church in the manifest hope of finding a replacement person, a surrogate father or mother, for the children. Parents Without Partners, a national organization with local groups in many cities, offers assistance in this direction.* Yet, churches as churches can form such ongoing groups of one-spouse parents, including widows, widowers, and divorcées, for mutual support.

The observant pastor, noting that divorcées tend to form natural subgroups anyway, can sometimes learn about these from the community grapevine. Informal social gatherings in homes are not unusual. How ingenious can a pastor be in getting invited into such gatherings for conversation? On two or three occasions it has happened serendipitously for me, without effort on my part. However, my more direct attempts to get parish pastors related to these groups have been unsuccessful—not, I think, because the groups have rejected the pastor as a person, but because they felt themselves to be outsiders so far as the church is concerned.

Stage 7: Post-divorce bereavement. Denial, anger, bargaining, despair and acceptance, the experiences of which Kübler-Ross speaks concerning anticipatory grief, apply to the process of separation leading up to divorce.† The process tends to be "recycled," however, after the social reality of the legal decree becomes a fact. Indeed, these experiences may be intensified—are certainly further complicated—by several factors.

First, the financial drain of a divorce can draw heavily on the pocketbook of the divorcée. Recovery from this aspect of the procedure may take years, not just months.

Second, if the couple lived in a community or a milieu oriented to traditional values and patterns in marriage and family living and they are suddenly thrust into a kind of no-man's-land or no-woman's-land, where they must struggle with the resultant "status break," for the divorced person the feeling is often one of "sliding" *down* the social ladder. Divorcées frequently move from a house to an apartment, or from a so-called good neighborhood to a not-so-good neighborhood. Club memberships often are no longer open to them and a subtle stigma may even jeopardize their job security or chances for advancement. The church's negative attitude toward divorce is one of the heaviest sanctions against them. William Goode found that a large number of divorcées in the Detroit area simply vanished from their communities and could not be located.* They went elsewhere and started over again. Many divorced people, especially where no children were involved, revert to calling themselves "single" and leave the term *divorced* off the official papers, records, forms, and applications. I personally think that this preference to be regarded legally as single should be honored as a matter of civil rights, once the marriage contract has been dissolved.

Third, hasty remarriage can impede and confuse the grief process which should follow a divorce as surely as it follows the loss of a significant other by death. This grief process needs to run its course. To obstruct it is to add a psychological burden to the new marriage, an additional hazard over and above those that we said (above, in stage 4) could attend the transformation of an affair into an early remarriage.

These three complicating factors in the grief process after divorce can best be handled in a growth group where feelings are openly expressed. The leader should consciously help all the members to examine the real feelings at each stage, and to do so within the context of the group as a new life support system. Persons should be encouraged to make as clean a break as possible from their divorced spouses. Their fantasies in their waking hours and their dreams at night can be explored, expressed, relived, and told good-bye. Their self-recriminations formulated in "iffy" hypothesizing, can be tested against the reality of the group. Their own part in the marital collapse can be realistically assessed, without the self-imposition of excessive burdens of guilt. Indeed, tenderness of heart and openness unprejudiced self-evaluation and new learning can be the hard-earned gains of a person who has suffered loss by divorce, but then been helped to grow in and through the experience.

Pastoral-Theological Concerns

The crucial questions that the pastor cannot dodge arise when divorced persons come and ask to be married again: "My former spouse is still alive. Will we then be living in sin? Will I be causing my new spouse to commit adultery?" The real issue here, for pastors who take their learnings from the Bible, is this: To whom was Jesus addressing his "difficult to bear" teaching? My interpretation is that he was addressing it to his disciples; he was not challenging the validity of Moses' teaching for the general population. Jesus' disciples once expressed the opinion that if a person were to follow his teachings it would be better not to marry at all. His response, all too often ignored, is worth pondering: "Not all men can receive this precept, but only those to whom it is given."

Not all people who come to the pastor have been turned from unteachableness to teachableness. Not all who seek remarriage even profess to have had a distinctly Christian marriage before. In a time when the separation of church and state was an unknown concept, Jesus gave us a teaching concerning the intention of God in creation for the mystical union of men and women in the one-flesh relationship of marriage. Christian pastors espouse that ideal for marriage. Yet we are called upon as men and women of unclean lips to minister to a people of unclean lips. Civil marriage contracts are formed today between men and women who have no knowl-

edge of Christian faith or biblical teaching, much less a commitment to Christian living. Even in the case of committed
Christians who regard their divorce as inevitable—the only
responsible course to take—we have to ask ourselves: Was
Jesus pointing to remarriage as *the* unpardonable sin? When
we judge his difficult-to-bear teaching by the rest of what we
know of Jesus, then we have to temper it by his saying to the
adulterous woman, "Go, and sin no more." Immediately we
begin, as did the early church, to look for extenuating circum-
stances. From the beginning Christians pointed to such
things as sexual cohabitation with another person, being
"unequally yoked together" so far as Christian commitment is
concerned, or total and long-term abandonment. We may
even see remarriage as the lesser of two evils, for example, in
the case of widows and widowers: "It is better to marry than
to be aflame with passion." Finally, those persons who simply
do not want to stay married need to bear in mind that the New
Testament does not condemn divorce, but only challenges
remarriage.

In group discussions, pastors can take a series of sessions
for dialogue about all the various teachings of the whole Bible
on the subjects of sexuality, marriage, divorce, and remarriage.* Much superstition exists about these teachings, even
among the clergy. Single quotations are often ripped out of
the setting in which they were spoken. Abysmal ignorance
prevails about the fact that divorce at the time of Jesus was a
male right, and that by the same law the woman had no rights.
The historical filters placed by one religious group after another on the whole counsel of the Scriptures have kept us
today at a low level of awareness with respect to the biblical
counsel on divorce and remarriage. Destructive legalism has
been the result. Serious study of the whole range of teachings
on divorce and remarriage can be creative rather than destructive. For example, the central biblical concept of forgiveness
is too quickly deleted from much contemporary interpretation.
Then, too, the writers of the Epistles, who must surely have
faced the problem, do not even mention divorce or remarriage
directly.

Inevitably such discussions of the biblical witness about marriage, divorce, and remarriage raise issues about the inherent equality of men and women in the sight of God as participants in the image of God in marriage, and in redemption. In the beginning we were made in the image of God as male and female. In marriage, we two became one flesh. In redemption in Christ there is neither male nor female. A straightforward biblical study group, rightly led, can become a consciousness-raising group in which the identity of men and women before God is the issue. For example, the curses placed upon man and woman in Genesis 3:16ff. can be viewed alongside such passages as Ephesians 5:25–31, 1 Peter 3:7, and 1 Corinthians 7:5. Such a comparison can lead to dramatic results in opening up the consciousness of a couples group to new experiences of the "otherness" of the sexes. The "submission passage" in Ephesians 5:22–24, for example, is often used as a "proof-text" by some interpreters, while others prefer to cite Ephesians 5:25–28 instead. The whole passage needs to be taken into consideration, with no part ignored.

Creative growth can take place where groups of divorcées come together for sharing and mutual support. Learning from their past griefs, even by trial and error, can lead to the kind of openness and teachableness of which an effective marriage is made. But, as Jesus said, not all people will go along with this.

3. Acute Grief and Separation

Anticipatory grief hovers with a seeming endlessness over the patient suffering from cancer, leukemia, or one of other slow killer diseases; the prospect of death affects the attending family as well. Likewise, chronic marriage conflict, spread over months or years of indecision and marked by rising and falling hopes, gives rise to a similar slow grief. Both involve in a grief process that is normal, necessary, and potentially a source of new strength and growth. In the previous chapter we spoke of such anticipatory grief; whether connected with death or with divorce, it needs to run its course.

We come now in the present chapter to deal with acute grief and separation, the sudden and unexpected kind that is more likely to be associated with death than with divorce so far as our two continuing paradigms are concerned.

The Grief Process in Sudden Death

A twenty-two year old college girl is driving happily along the freeway. Her small car is suddenly sideswiped by a careening truck whose driver is drunk. There is a crash. The car bursts into flames. The girl is burned to death in a matter of seconds.

A ten year old boy is on his way home from school. He grabs a favorite limb on a favorite tree for a happy-go-lucky swing. The limb swerves in an unexpected direction and throws him off into the street, directly into the path of an oncoming vehicle. He is instantly crushed under the wheels of the car.

Psychophysiological Responses

In instances such as these involving sudden death, Kübler-Ross says that the bereaved family moves through the cycle of denial, anger, bargaining, despair, and acceptance in much the same way that the family of a slowly dying patient does prior to the death. I would like to take exception to this assumption and identify several factors that her formula does not include:

Shock. The element of suddenness produces a qualitatively different kind of shock than does the more easily denied "slow death," and shock unhinges the psychophysiological machinery of life. Shock, physiologically defined, is "a clinical condition characterized by signs and symptoms which arise when the cardiac output is insufficient to fill the arterial tree with blood under sufficient pressure to provide organs with adequate blood flow."*

The person who receives the sudden news, for example, of the death of his daughter in a burning automobile immediately becomes in a sense an active heart patient. The shock involved in hearing such a message could produce a radical heart reaction. If at all possible, his physician should be present when he is told the news. A pastor can see to it that his physician is notified. Denial and disbelief are certainly present, but the attendant shock involves far more than the mere psychodynamic of denial; the person reacts as if physically hit, stunned, by a blow with a heavy object.

Panic. At the psychological level panic is the correlate of the physiological state of shock. Panic frequently follows receipt of the sudden news of the death of a loved one. It needs to be handled. Jurgen Ruesch says that the management of a situation in which panic develops is dependent upon the emergence of a leader.† Not infrequently the pastor fills that bill. Hospital chaplains emerge regularly from emergency rooms as the leader in managing a panicked family who has just been told that their loved one was "dead on arrival." Similarly chaplains and parish pastors frequently stand vigil with the waiting family during what was at the outset expected to be a routine operation, only to find that when the operation suddenly reverses and the patient dies they are called upon to deal with a similar panic situation.

Several procedures are imperative in dealing with panic:

First, the pastor must exercise firm, clear leadership and have his/her own anxiety under control. Panic is contagious. Don't "catch" it.

Second, because panic is contagious the pastor should move quickly to isolate the panicked person from the other persons, lest the others tend to "catch" it as well. It is good strategy to move the individual to a family waiting room or conference room or chapel in the hospital, or to another room of the house if the panic scene occurs at home.

Third, avoid asking questions and concentrate on simple commands such as: "Let's sit down here for a minute." "Now let's walk around just a little." "You've had the breath knocked out of you, breathe as deeply as you can." If the person smokes, you may offer a cigarette and light it. If the room seems too cold or too warm a coat or sweater or jacket may be put on (or taken off) the panicked individual.

Someone can be asked to bring a warm drink—perhaps coffee, tea, or hot chocolate—to the person in shock or panic. The pastor can sit with the person as he or she drinks. I recall sitting in an orphanage with a ten year old boy whose brother had drowned. I took him aside, away from the rest of the children, and sat with him in the kitchen as we drank some hot chocolate together.

Some persons, when they hear shocking news, will actually faint or seem to faint. I saw one woman faint three times within the first hour after the death of her husband in an industrial accident. Each time she revived we told her again in a brief and matter-of-fact way what had happened. Her physician was with us as we did so.

Shock and panic may recur intermittently for as long as two to five days and the person so affected should be monitored both pastorally and medically throughout this period. Such psychophysiological response to trauma is more than a mere psychological defense mechanism reinforcing various forms of denial. It calls for medical attention and perhaps treatment.

Numbness. In my experience persons who have suddenly

lost a loved one by death usually suffer a curious psychophysiological state of numbness after the initial shock and panic
subside. They complain of not being able to feel, of not feeling close to people or to God, of not knowing how to respond.
They often rub their hands, arms, foreheads, or necks as if
they were anesthetized—as if parts of the body had "gone to
sleep" on them. Feelings of coldness are not at all unusual.
When talking to a pastor, the bereaved may put these feelings into theological language: "I just don't feel like praying
anymore." As Tennyson, in his grief over the death of his
friend, Arthur Henry Hallam, wrote:

> But, for the unquiet heart and brain
> A use in measured language lies;
> The sad mechanic exercise,
> Like dull narcotics, numbing pain.*

These states—shock, panic, and numbness—tend to pre-
cede the return of such feelings as denial, anger, and resent-
ment. Very religious people may loudly and instantly protest
their forgiveness and love: they bear no ill will whatever toward the deceased—or toward the persons responsible for the
death, such as the drunken truck driver. But they "protest
too much." Here Kübler-Ross's emphasis upon denial is extremely appropos. However, denial as a cognitive experience
is initially submerged in a tidal wave of shock, panic, and
numbness such as I have sought to describe.

Fantasy Formation

After the initial stages of shock and numbness have worn
off various kinds of fantasy formations take place in the bereaved person's response to traumatic loss. These fantasy
formations resembled the "phantom limb" experience of the
amputee who has lost an arm or a leg. So far as the mind-set
is concerned, the attachment continues. A person continues
to "reach out" as if a deceased love one were still there. The
wife of a deceased husband may continue to set his place at
the dinner table for him. The husband of a suddenly de-

ceased wife may go home expecting dinner to be ready. We can call this "force of habit" if we wish; habits of course are not easily reprogrammed, and behavior modification counselors have shown that a set of habits developed over a lifetime or over a period of many years have to be reconditioned and reinforced with the new data:* "Your loved one is dead." Yet the psychoanalytic data cannot be discounted: there is a point where such behavior ceases to be just a habit and becomes as well witting or unwitting maintenance of a satisfying fantasy.

For example, some persons simply do not struggle with the reality of the death. They capitulate to fantasy. They will maintain the room of the deceased just as it was, or they will enshrine a picture of the deceased. When August Comte, the founder of the school of philosophy known as logical positivism, lost his beloved mate Clothilde, he maintained the fantasy of her presence by organizing a group of close friends who would meet regularly to reenact the memories of Clothilde; it became almost a Clothilde cult. Indeed, worship of the dead is not at all unusual in both primitive and sophisticated religions.

The gestalt therapists have chosen to light a candle rather than curse the darkness of fantasy formations.† In the loving context of a support group or of an individual counseling relationship, they suggest the discipline of getting in touch with lost persons in one's life through a guided fantasy experience. The whole relationship of unresolved problems between the living and the dead is explored, aired, negotiated, and concluded in the language of hypothesis. In short, the person is encouraged to act, think, and speak *as if* the deceased were actually sitting in an empty chair or lying on an empty couch. The group session or the individual counseling session is used to encourage persons to say and do the things they would in fact wish to say and do if the deceased were actually sitting there.

The process going on here is referred to as "abreaction." Abreaction means to let loose or discharge emotions connected with an idea, fact, or memory. In a reenactment set-ting the person relives and works through to the reality of the loved one's death. This is not done alone but in the com-panionship of an individual counselor or a life support group. The objective is to break through to and get in touch with the reality of the loss, to own up to any *present* feelings of anger, abandonment, or guilt, and tenderness, love, or unexpressed gratitude with respect to the deceased. For many people, Hamlet-like relationship to the deceased is realistic so far as their experience of grief is concerned. The aim of such guided fantasy experience is to let the dead rest in peace, "bury their dead" so to speak.

One of the characteristic phenomena of traumatic, sudden loss by death is that the person never gets to bid the loved one farewell. In longer-term, more slow-acting forms of death, this leave taking occurs more often, although not always in any definitive way. Therefore either at a group or individual level, the pastoral counselor can encourage the bereaved per-son to say in words what would have been said had there been opportunity to tell the deceased good-bye. This can be done through role play with another individual in the group or with the group leader. Such leave taking is a part of the continu-ing struggle to come to grips with the reality of the loss. Its goal is to bring a satisfying sense of closure to a significant relationship that must now end where it was and be moved to another level of meaning and perception.

Grieving and Tears

Many persons will attest that they never were able to cry at the time of their loved one's death. They may have wanted to cry many times since but have been unable to do so. The stage of "despair" of which Kübler-Ross speaks is often ac-companied by a release of emotion that is accompanied by tears. A physiological response of the whole body to the experience of loss is involved in the shedding of tears. The person who does not cry at first viewing the corpse, at the funeral, at the graveside, or even earlier at the first news of the death is often the person generally regarded as the "king-pin" of the family organization. Such persons are said to "hold up so well." They are often reinforced in this by those around them. Religion is often invoked as a force which enables people to bear pain and loss stoically, with no expression of emotion. Sometimes this ability is even extolled as a religious virtue. Not so! Sooner or later such emotions will come out, if not in one form then in another.

Usually in the case of a traumatic bereavement the flood of tears and despair comes later. For this reason a pastor is well advised to "double back," making repeated visits to the bereaved for as much as a month to six months later. As a chaplain and professor, I normally have little responsibility for the formal aspects of the care of the bereaved. My most effective ministry to close associates and counselees who have lost someone by death occurs some time after the funeral. I seek to enable mourners to pour out their grief. Parish pastors can assist in this way as well, not just at the time of the death and funeral but in continuing visits for some time thereafter.

This catharsis may take the form of a "complaint against God." The Psalms are full of such prayers of complaint. Hannah, who was grieved because she could not have children, told Eli that she was "pouring out her complaint before the Lord." The pastoral way to growth for the bereaved is to enable them to do just this: pour out their complaint. In praying with bereaved persons, I often affirm their feelings by giving thanks to God for being the kind of God who can hear with understanding not only our praise and thanksgiving, but also our complaints of injustice and our laments of insensitivity, yet not destroy us. In my experience the fruits of such honesty is not destruction but new growth. After all, by letting God know how we really feel, we are not adding to God's knowledge of us; we are simply getting in touch with what God already knows about us, with ourselves as we really are. As we do so God accepts and affirms us, providing fresh growth and new strength for living today.

Selective Memory

A catharsis of tears and despair is normally, at the level of conscious awareness, a predictable prelude to a sort of ennui, a lassitude. Sleep becomes the natural and God-given agent enabling a person to grow through despair. The daily life of the grief-stricken person begins to slip back to normal. There is less preoccupation with the past, more capacity to concentrate on the present, renewed ability to take initiative and to make decisions. As far as possible, major decisions should in fact be delayed until these cognitive abilities return.

Yet, this superficial return to normalcy is punctuated by events that reactivate the mourning process at the level of conscious memory. A missionary couple expelled from China after the Communist takeover returned to the United States on a ship named the *Gripsholm*. Several months after her husband's death, the widow was taken to a luncheon at the Gripsholm Restaurant in New York. The name of the restaurant took her by complete surprise. As she got out of a taxi, looked up at the marquee, and saw the word *Gripsholm*, she stopped suddenly and caught her breath as if struck by something physical. She paused a moment and then exclaimed: "My husband and I came home on the *Gripsholm!*"

Events that trigger selective memory may initiate a mini-process of mourning that can last for two or three days. The person will feel pensive and sad, with no definable reason for doing so. As Tennyson further described his feelings about his deceased friend:

> Yet feels, as in a pensive dream,
> When all his active powers are still,
> A distant dearness in the hill,
> A secret sweetness in the stream.*

These periods of reflectiveness and heavyheartedness tend to become less frequent with the passage of time, and for a reason: Each person, place, thing, activity, event, item on the daily agenda of a person's life must eventually be associated with the present reality: "My loved one is dead." These items are innumerable to begin with, but their number is gradually whittled down as day by day they are associated with new realities in one's present life. As this happens, habits of thought and behavior are being reconditioned.

Bereavement Dreams

As the process of selective memory renegotiates life for the individual at the conscious level, so the bereavement dream does the same thing at the more unconscious level of existence.

Sigmund Freud writes:

> When a man has lost someone dear to him, for a considerable period afterwards he produces a special type of dream, in which the most remarkable compromises are effected between his knowledge that that person is dead and his desire to call him back to life. Sometimes the deceased is dreamt of as being dead, and yet still alive because he does not know that he is dead, as if he would only really die if he did know it; at other times he is half dead and half alive, and each of these conditions has its distinguishing marks. We must not call these dreams merely nonsensical.*

A Vietnam soldier told me very recently that whereas he was in combat and lost friends by death all around him during the years 1968–69 it was not until the spring of 1974 that he could remember dreaming about his combat experiences. The bereavement dream, says Waller and Hill, "seems to take us straight to the heart of the conflict over death. . . .   The knowing mind, which is in contact with reality, receives the impression of death and records it; the mental system which deals with reality accepts this knowledge.   But there is a part of us which does not immediately accept this verdict.   There is a wishful mental system which will not give up.   There is a desire not to accept the ultimate frustration of death."†

The sharing of dreams about one's deceased and lost loved ones in individual and group counseling is important as a regular exercise in memory.   The pastor can share his or her own dreams of persons loved and lost.   I can share one of mine here.

I was in Glendale, California recently for some lectures. My hosts took me one afternoon to tour the elaborate Forest Lawn Cemetery nearby. Its mingled patterns of sentimental religion, ardent patriotism, and near worship of the dead were rationally offensive to me. I could not "see" spending all that money and real estate on the dead when so many of the living are in such a dire plight. It reminded me of my poverty background and of how my later rationalisms called for a better ecology, a wiser stewardship of money, and a religion of great adventure rather than the nostalgia of the worship of the dead.

That night, however, I dreamed about my grandmother long deceased. She had been the beloved person who cared for me as an infant and child while my mother worked. Now in my dream we were having her funeral all over again. I dreamed that I personally had arranged it all, a $10,000 funeral, including a real Irish wake! Everyone had a great time —even my grandmother, who was dead, and yet not dead. It was her funeral we were having, but she too was there to enjoy the festivities, all the beauty, all the luxury that I had provided!

In actuality my grandmother died during the Great Depression. We hardly had enough money to bury her the least expensive way. There was even conflict over who would pay the expenses. I was old enough at the time to know all that was going on. Now, it was as if the dream was an undoing of all this privation, an attempt at overdoing the funeral. My dream was obviously plugged into the previous day's experience at the plush Forest Lawn Cemetery. What was amazing to me, though, was that after all these years, I would dream a classical wish fulfillment dream about my grandmother.

I also associate this dream with a recent experience in present reality: An elderly woman to whom I had been deeply related over a period of twenty-five years, recently rejected me outright because I changed jobs. I find myself wondering whether the more recent grief over this personal rejection may not be what reactivated former grief over my grandmother. I also wonder if the dream itself was not a form of denial of the more recent grief as well as a reactivation of the older grief: my elderly friend is about the same age now as my grandmother was at the time of her death.

I have shared my dream here, and my thoughts about it, in order to illustrate the pattern of conversation which pastors can initiate in a group of persons who are bereaved and seeking to grow through grief to hope and new levels of maturity. To dream with your group is to enter upon a creative process. Do not look for hidden meanings; simply lay out the ones that are apparent. Encourage group members to articulate the meanings that come easily and spontaneously to mind. The plain meaning of the dream rests in the thoughts of the person who dreamed it. The dreamers themselves are the best interpreters of their own dreams and their meaning *to them*. The pastor/leader does not have to assume that burden.

A New Reason For Being

The grief process is not really complete until the bereaved persons work through to the discovery of a new purpose for life and a fresh reason for being independent of the deceased. They make the decision "to live again," as Catherine Marshall puts it in the title of her book about how she finally decided to "give up" Peter Marshall and to live again.* This decision may occur in connection with entry upon a new line of work. It may accompany reinvestment of life in a younger generation, in grandchildren, or students, or little children who are without families of their own. The discovery of a new reason for being often occurs at the point of remarriage after the death or divorce of a spouse. In any event, the grief process I have described must run its course until it culminates in the discovery of a new purpose for living.

Recurrent Themes of Mourning

The process of grief described in the foregoing pages may seem clear-cut and well-packaged, but it is not so neat in reality. Phases overlap each other. Individuals take two steps forward and one step backward along the way. There are also variations in the typical grief process, such as delayed grief and pathological grief, and we shall speak of these in more detail in the next chapter. Suffice it to say here that several themes of emotion run through the process of grief in all its variations, and these can and need to be sensed, felt, recognized, and articulated in pastoral care of the bereaved.

The Feeling of Injustice

The feeling of having been treated unjustly is a predominant motif in grief. It elicits feelings of anger.

The bereaved may say that if the medical care of the deceased had been wiser, better, different, or quicker, then the loved one would not have died. Thus, they are likely to feel cheated by the physicians—and angry about it too. They may feel that God has dealt cruelly with them in taking their loved one from their midst and allowing them to be left alone. Thus they may express anger toward the past, even toward God.

Anger is a natural reaction to the feeling of injustice, whether real or perceived. Particularly among religious people, who share a heavy taboo against angry feelings, I find that talking with them about their sense of injustice elicits expressions of anger without immediately mobilizing their resistance to the idea of seeing themselves as "angry" people. One of the great values of dealing with bereaved persons in support groups is that through simulation games, sympathetic imagination, and empathic responses by other group members who may not have such inhibitions about anger, persons can be helped to vent and even to acknowledge this powerful and potentially destructive emotion.

The Illusion of Immortality

Freud once said that all of us unconsciously believe we will never die. The illusion is fostered as long as we live by cultural denial, subgroup denial, and personal denial of death.

However, for all of us "it is just a matter of time" before we die. Realizing this fact makes each one of us, regardless of age, uncomfortable; and coming to terms with the idea is not easy. Admitting and accepting the death of a loved one shatters—at least for the time being—any illusions we may have about ourselves. This is why in the grief process at every stage, the persistent illusion of immortality in this life is a recurrent theme.

Idolatry of the Dead

Pathological grief sets in when the bereaved over-idealizes the deceased to such an extent that the lost loved one for all practical purposes takes on the attributes of a god. Sometimes the bereaved will even center their lives around their loss of the beloved. Where this becomes a fixed pattern, there develops at best a religion of nostalgia centered upon the past, or at worst a pathological grief state.

The central theological affirmation in such a situation is that God is a God of the living and not of the dead—indeed that *God*, not the deceased, is God! As Proust says, "In our mourning for the dead we pay idolatrous worship to the things they liked."* Edna St. Vincent Millay's "Lament" articulates the more realistic view, even despite the hurt which the parent must feel:

> Life must go on,
> And the dead be forgotten;
> Life must go on,
> Though good men die;
> Anne, eat your breakfast;
> Dan, take your medicine;
> Life must go on;
> I forget just why.†

Traumatic Divorce

Clinically speaking, I have observed "sudden revelations" of a collapsing marriage in which a partner, seemingly without any previous notice whatsoever, suddenly finds himself or herself on the verge of initiating immediate divorce procedures, or having them initiated by the spouse. The number of these instances has been so rare, however, that I cannot generalize about the after-traumatic reactions.

In the three cases that I have observed in thirty years of pastoral work, the elements of shock, panic, numbness, and fantasy-formation already described were definitely present. They were remarkably similar to the grief reactions attendant upon death. In one instance, the person refused all help, while going for fifteen years from one marriage counselor to another trying to get them to make her husband come back to her.

My major observation about divorce as a crisis involving acute grief is that for the person experiencing such sudden marital rupture, denial and fantasy-formation is probably a well-established way of life that long antedated the marriage itself. To be out of touch with one's mate's real self and activities long enough for a divorce to be almost a foregone conclusion before one even suspects it calls for massive denial, extreme naiveté, or a dreamy way of life, or all three. Such a stance toward life does exist in some individuals, but it is certainly the exception rather than the rule. Ordinarily, I would conclude, divorce involves the longer anticipatory kind of grief described in the previous chapter. Sudden marital separation or divorce is more often an evidence of chronically withdrawn patterns of relationships. Occasionally an impulse decision to leave one's spouse is made by a seriously depressed person, even as a seriously depressed person may sometimes suddenly walk off the job, or jeopardize his or her job or community status by bizarre patterns of behavior, perhaps a sudden romance with some unlikely person.

When such cases come to a pastor's attention medical consultation is indicated. Delaying procedures should be used to slow the complementation of the decision. If at all possible, the person or persons should be urged to make another appointment each time they are seen either individually, conjointly, or in a group. They can be asked to enter upon what in Transactional Analysis terms is called a "contract," *not* to make a marital decision to divorce one's spouse or a vocational decision to quit one's job until a longer, more reflective kind of counseling can take place.*   Admittedly, such procedures are of a "first aid" variety, but the goal of such first aid is to conserve as much of the life and potential of the marriage and the person as is possible and at the same time to "free up" the reflective processes in the person's life to make a considered rather than an impulsive decision.

4. Varieties of Grief and Separation

Our previous chapters assumed the kind of grief that is the result of deep attachment to the person lost. The grief process we described would normally take from one to two years to run its course, although vestiges of the grief could remain indefinitely in the case of the deeper attachments. We also assumed that opportunities existed for the grief to be expressed and worked through in a creative way, enabling the person to grow in and through the experience of loss and ultimately to arrive at a fresh new reason for being and a deeper empathy for other bereaved pesons.

These assumptions, of course, do not hold in all instances. There are variations of the grief process that call for separate treatment in their own right, lest the pastoral counselor find himself or herself "forcing" the bereaved person into this relatively reliable but necessarily preconceived pattern. The pastor will inevitably encounter grief situations that simply do not fit the usual pattern. We need, therefore, to ask, What are some of the variables that produce a different kind of grief reaction to loss and separation? and What are some of the major grief reactions that differ in kind from the typical process thus far described?

Variables in the Grief Occasioned by Death

The Length of the Relationship

Shared experiences of life accumulate in the memory. Persons who experience significant loss through death or other forms of separation inevitably need to work through these memories. Indeed, the process of grief is in large measure a matter of reminiscence.

Ordinarily, the longer a person has known someone, the more such experiences they have shared together and the greater the sense of loss on the part of the grieving person. The elderly couple, for example, who have lived together so closely for so long that often each can accurately anticipate what the other is thinking, tend to lose awareness of boundaries that divide them as persons. When one of them dies, the other may follow—perhaps out of grief—in death very soon. By contrast, for newlyweds who have been married only a few months—or even a year or two—the blending of personalities is not so great and the grief reaction probably less destructive.

The Quality of the Relationship

Not all deaths are unwelcome. A wife has been extremely ill for two years. Her husband provides basic minimal care. At the same time, however, he has a mistress, and they seem to be "waiting around" for the legal wife to die. Kübler-Ross tells of one case in her sample research where the family felt that the sooner the patient died the better things would be.* Relationships can be so superficial or uncaring that death comes as relief, even as a wish realized. Often it is the quality of the relationship that will determine the quantity and quality of grief. A negative relationship may produce little or no grief at death, or perhaps only a morbid grief reaction involving inappropriate guilt.

On the other hand, the quality of the relationship may be one of serene respect and unswerving devotion. It may be one involving open communication and realistic joint planning for the future. Death in such instances can alter the character and depth of the grief.

The whole spectrum of human relationships is open to pastoral evaluation as to the various shades of meaning death may hold for those who mourn the deceased. For example, the degree of kinship alone is not a reliable index for estimating the meaning of a death for the survivors. The death of a grandmother, a cousin, an aunt, or an older sister may actually mean more to a bereaved person than that of a father or mother.   The pastor needs to explore the whole question of relationship, not simply as to duration but also as to quality and kind: "Were you close to your grandmother?"   "Did you grow up with your grandfather near you?"   "How long have you been living on your own away from your folks?"

Timeliness and Untimeliness in Grief

Another variable in the grief process is the degree of timeliness or untimeliness in the death.   For example, grief over an elderly person who has lived long and well and finally "lies down to pleasant dreams" in death is a kind of grief that is mingled with celebration of a life well-lived.   Grief for a young person who has just finished. the long grind of medical school, practiced for a year, and then dies of a fast-working cancer presents a different kind of grief in which there is little sense of celebration.

Death by freak accident is an untimely death.   A young husband and father is suddenly burned to death after carelessly catching his clothes on fire at a barbecue grill on the patio.   If *only* he had had the good sense not to try starting a fire with gasoline!   Grief in such cases tends to focus on the needlessness, senselessness, absurdity, and waste.

The Nature of the Death

The nature or manner of death is unquestionably an important determinant of the grief process.   Till now we have distinguished between the anticipatory grief attendant upon a slow, insiduous death or divorce procedure and the traumatic acute grief connected with a sudden, unexpected loss.   Within these two major categories more specific distinctions can of course be made:

The death that mutilates or destroys the body.   Combat in war often is such as to annihilate the bodies of the fighting men.   Death in explosion or fire often is the equivalent of cremation for the victims.   This is also true for some who die in plane or auto crashes.   Where death so mutilates or de-

stroys the body as to prevent the mourners from actually seeing their deceased loved ones, natural questions arise: "Is she
really dead or is someone just telling me that that unrecogniz-
able pile of charred remains is my daughter?"   "Is that really
my son in the flag-draped box or did they send someone else's
body back from the war?"   "This whole thing may be somebody's cruel mistake."   Positive identification of the body can
often help significantly in a mourner's acceptance of the reality of death.

The suicide.   The self-inflicted death complicates the grief
process in exceptional ways.   The mourner probes for reasons
why the deceased would do this: "Was she mentally ill?"
"Was he angry at me?"   "Was it something I did that trig-
gered it?"   "How could my beloved deliberately leave me with
all these responsibilities to bear alone?"   Relatives will occasionally blame each other.   Parents of the deceased tend to
blame the surviving spouse: "If only he or she had taken better care of our child, this suicide would never have happened."
When the grief is honestly faced, it becomes clear that no
one person can watch over another twenty-four hours a day,
that each of us is responsible for only one life—our own.
This is a harsh reality, but to realize it can be healing in the
long run.   A person can learn to grieve over a suicide without
feeling guilty, although a majority of persons *do* feel guilty.*

Theological questions arise out of the ancient notion that
suicide represents an unrepented sin—unrepentable and
therefore unpardonable.   This superstition overlooks the
grace of God, however, as the source of forgiveness.   It is
God's grace, not man's repentance, that removes the guilt of
any sin.   Repentance is not a *work* that a person *performs* in
order to *earn* salvation and forgiveness.   Such "steel trap
logic" about forgiveness being through repentance alone is a
snare for the mourners of a person who has committed suicide.   The love of Christ is calculated to overrule such superstition and set them free.

When suicide is complicated by a preceding divorce or
threat of divorce, the separation already in effect at the time of

the death compounds the ensuing grief. The ultimate in tragedy, however, is when a person kills other members of the family and then commits suicide. The qualitative difference in a grief occasioned by suicide may be further accentuated by the fear of the survivors that they themselves—or their offsprings—for hereditary or other inevitable reasons are also likely to "end up" in suicide. The whole issue of individual differences is often obscured by "scare" statistics, pontifical pronouncements about heredity, and the misuse of medical and psychiatric data by unreflective persons. The law of statistical averages simply does not apply in specific cases.

Variables in the Grief Attendant Upon Divorce

I have been speaking of variables in the process of grief occasioned by death. Similar variables appear in the separation attendant upon divorce. They need to be mentioned as well.

The Length of Marriage

Statistics on the frequency of divorce huddle around the third year of marriage. The depth of acrimony and bitterness —and grief—is not as great in these "lightly invested" marriages as in longer marriages. Especially poignant is the suffering, for example, of a wife who "slaved" for years to put her husband through professional school only to be deserted by him when he sets up his practice and becomes "successful." Heavily invested, even overinvested marriages that end in divorce have a longer and more stringent grief process.

The Presence or Absence of Children

Divorce ought to be a definitive ending of a relationship. The couple with younger children, however, have a much more indecisive divorce relationship than the couple without children. Shared time spent with the children usually reactivates conflict between the parents. The finances of child support become a festering problem. It is one thing to say:

"Make a clean break of your relationship in a divorce." It is another thing to be able to do this if one spouse has the children all winter and the other has them all summer, or if one has the children one weekend and the other has them the next. The resulting stress and conflict can stretch out over a lifetime.

Somewhere the tension has to snap. Often the break comes when one or the other spouse simply abdicates all further relationship to the children. This often happens at the point of remarriage, particularly when the second spouse—the new parent—begins to develop a relationship of trust and respect with the children.

The Degree of Poverty or Affluence

Extreme poverty and extreme wealth both present variants in the grief process which attends separation and divorce. In many instances exceptionally poor persons simply desert the marriage. Later liaisons tend to be common-law relationships at best. The provision of aid to dependent children by welfare agencies may affect the motives for separation. The husband may move back into or out of the relationship sporadically. The wife may have her mother serve as baby-sitter while she herself works to get off of welfare. Without someone like a mother or an older daughter available to baby-sit the wife and mother in poverty may waver back and forth between welfare and various kinds of negotiations with men who will help her survive, among them her ex-husband.

The affluent couple who divorce have different but equally chronic grief over their separateness. Money may have been the point of greatest conflict in their marriage. "Division" of their money and property can also be the source of greatest friction during and long after the divorce proceedings.

Resulting Varieties of Grief and Separation

We have discussed some of the many variables in grief and separation. We can now specify the several kinds of grief and

separation that have been distinguished in terms of the resulting reactions.*

Chronic Grief

Grief is a normal part of the growing life but it can also
stalemate into a chronic way of life if a person fails to move
through the process in a normal way. So far as our relationship to other persons is concerned, we have no *ultimately* sure
dwelling place. Persons to whom we may have been related
in depth and elevation over a period of twenty, thirty, even
forty years can—for reasons over which we have no control—
become alienated from us almost in an instant. The grief of
such a break is then ever before us. Yet the words of the
gospel hymn come back to remind us: "The arm of flesh will
fail you, you dare not trust your own."† Jesus called attention to the fragility and earthboundness even of marriage
when he said: "In the resurrection, there will be neither marriage nor giving in marriage." If ultimate hope is placed in
penultimate relationships, chronic grief is bound to be the result. But if we can learn to accept human fallibility with a
measure of serenity and humor there is always the possibility
of growth and the fuller realization of human potential precisely in the face of grief and separation.

Delayed Grief

Bereaved and estranged people are sometimes so activistic
and preoccupied with peripheral concerns that they allow
themselves no time to grieve. They hasten pell-mell into new
causes, new work commitments, new life partnerships. They
have no time left to let down, let go, and give in to grief.
They never plumb the depths of their feelings of loss, except
perhaps when they later join a group established to encourage
growth and to elevate awareness. Hopefully, they will then
take the time to grieve, to open themselves prayerfully to the
concern and care of others, to overcome their need to pretend
and keep up a false front. In a loving community people can
often get in touch with their deepest and most authentic selves.

Pathological Grief

The grief attendant upon death and separation is crucial if growth on the part of the bereaved is to occur. The pathological fixations and regressions in grief and separation do take some bizarre forms; yet it would be wrong to build an understanding of grief as such, and of the great masses of bereaved persons, on the assumptions of pathology; that would be subtly to "program" people into thinking of grief as abnormal. Far from it: grief is a normal part of life, a necessary part of becoming an adult, of "putting away childish things."

For some few persons, however, life seems to come unhinged and be thrown into a clearly psychiatric state by grief. Such persons are far fewer than the psychiatric community would estimate, but *one* such person calls for and deserves the combined therapeutic teamwork of family physician, psychiatrist, and pastor. When a psychotic break is precipitated by grief or separation, emergency care is indicated. Such cases are the exception, however, rather than the rule, and realistic facing of the grief may be the pastor's best way of getting through to what is yet well in a sick patient. Andras Angyal was right in his theory of universal ambiguity: no person is *completely* sick, but is sustained at the same time by responsible and life-giving sources of health.* This is as sure in the case of a psychotic person as it is in the case of a feverish child suffering from an upper respiratory infection: both white blood cells and red blood cells are present and active in coping with the disease and in maintaining health simultaneously.

Ministering to Persons in Grief and Separation

We have classified the different kinds of grief and separation in terms of the grief process, the cause of death, and the quality of the prior relationships. Several strategic measures need also to be mentioned whereby the pastor's ministry to the grief-stricken can be enhanced.

Timing

The pastor who perceives grief as a process will be aware of the importance of "timing" the ministry to the mourner. Each mourner comes to grips with loss "in his or her own time." The pastor cannot gauge the propitious moment by a clock or a calendar, but only by the "fullness of time" for that particular person. Each human being has a personal *chronos* for grief.

Knowledge of the variables in each person's situation can be gained by listening, by careful inquiry, and by observation. There is no substitute, of course, for having already known the person to some extent *before* the loss. But sensing the fullness of time involves more than merely an "intuition." Empirical experience, hard data, and "technical know-how" are needed along with the charisma of "awareness" or "sensitivity."

Personal Coping

Many pastors regard grief in purely rational terms as an event that happens and is likely to end with the funeral. They perceive their ministry as one of "having the answers" and of being able to "dispel grief with word magic." This is totally unrealistic and unrealism may well be part and parcel of our all-pervading human and cultural propensity to deny the awesome forces we cannot foster or control: the harsh reality of death, the hardheartedness in human nature that lies behind divorce, the dark mystery of being that shrouds loss and separation of every kind. For pastors, such rationalism may be our own human coping device to help us avoid rather than face the ambiguities of human life as it is. Yet such static perceptions of grief leave the would-be counselor personally in a sweaty state of anxiety.

Learning to swim in the river of human process-in-time is itself an anxiety-provoking experience. The anxiety involved never ends; it is forever being mobilized, it can be disciplined, and it needs to be made productive. What is called for is the careful establishment of a longer-term counseling relationship. An extended program of visitation, telephoning, and contact with individual mourners of the deceased, or with individual divorced persons, is a more useful form of ministry for them as well as a form of continuing education for the pastor.

A supportive and sharing growth group made up of persons who have suffered the loss of significant people in their lives within a given year can often lead to the accumulation of two or three such groups in the span of two or three years. When such groups come together it's rarely necessary to "check" attendance; hungry people naturally cluster around good food. Such groups become a life support system for their members. The pastor who participates in such a group usually finds that it is not long until grief or loss strikes home personally. Then, with the comfort with which they themselves have been comforted, the group turns and comforts their leader.

Diversity of Communication

The pastor attempting to minister to people suffering from grief and separation may be overwhelmed by the demand unless he or she uses effectively all possible forms of communication. The casual contact on the street or at the shopping center is one such form. Another is the "after-meeting" conversations at the church. These can be significant moments of ministry when judiciously used. The written message—often in a handwritten letter—is a medium left in disuse by all too many pastors. The letter has advantages that a phone call or personal visit do not have: the person can read it in private, with no invasion of personal privacy by a voice or a body; the person can respond or not respond at will, with no subtle pressures requiring immediate reply; the person can read and reread, going over the contents of the letter again and again.

The telephone, of course, can and should be used to extend a pastor's ministry at propitious moments, for example, on the anniversary of a grief or separation. In dealing with members of the opposite sex, the telephone can be used to great advantage; it obviates the anxiety provocation that might be occasioned by a personal visit. The telephone also provides a kind of privacy that neither the psychoanalyst's couch nor the confessional booth provides. Indeed, the telephone is also such a good time-saver and gasoline saver that the pastor may be tempted to use it exclusively, as a substitute for personal visits and counseling interviews.*

Home visits with the bereaved normally and naturally cluster around the immediate crisis of death or divorce. My own suggestion is that a visit to the home at least monthly for the first three months after the crisis is a good guideline, though by no means a fixed rule. Gradually the person must be stimulated on his or her own initiative to "come to see" the pastor either for an individual conference or for a group session; covenanting to do this enables the person to convalesce from loss much more rapidly.†

It is important to use the whole pastoral spectrum of available resources. Being "locked in" to any one particular modality leads to frustration for the pastor and to a "threadbareness" of the one pastoral resource used.

One final observation about the use of pastoral resources could serve as the theme for a whole volume: Preaching too often tends to avoid altogether the realities of death and divorce. The pastor's sermons cannot "dwell" on these subjects, of course, but neither should a preacher ignore them altogether out of fear of being labeled a "deathbed" preacher. Effective death education from the pulpit and creative confrontation of the ambiguities of divorce in sermons can open the hearts of people and make them receptive to other forms of pastoral care and counseling. Where wisdom and compassion are combined in the preaching people are enabled to "make room in their hearts" for the pastor as a representative of that loving God who is always ready to care in time of grief and separation.

5. Pastoral Rituals in Grief and Separation

A ritual is a rite. It is a mutually agreed upon and commonly understood ceremony of consolation, celebration, and/or spiritual comradeship of a community with one or more of its members in time of need. A ritual tends to come into being when people in increasing numbers have to go through the same experience again and again. In the process they learn certain ways of doing so.

The processes of grief and separation are set within a flowing sequence of time. When a death, a marriage, a divorce, or a retirement occurs, the community either responds or fails to respond to the persons involved. In this process, there are, according to Arnold van Gennep, three kinds of rites or rituals: rites of separation, rites of transition, and rites of reentry or reincorporation into the community.* Examples of these rites may help to clarify their meaning and importance.

A typical rite of separation occurs, for example, when armed forces personnel are "mustered out" of the service. Another takes place when a young couple announce their engagement. In the instance of the military rite, people are "separated" from service. In the instance of the engaged couple they are "separated" from the ranks of the eligible males and females in the single population.

A typical rite of transition may be seen in the Jewish Bar Mitzvah, when a young Jewish boy is "carried over" by the community from the status of a child to that of an adult. Another rite of transition occurs in connection with marriage, as the wedding and honeymoon structure the movement from single status to that of a married couple.

A rite of reincorporation or reentry was normally provided for service personnel at war's end—after World War II, the Korean War, and the Vietnam War—in the form of the "G. I. Bill." The expectation was that a young person would return and enter upon or resume a college education. This particular rite "backfired" for the first large contingents of returning Vietnam veterans; they resisted, resented, and ignored attempts at a "hero's welcome" on campuses which had become the focus of anti-war protests.

The rite of reentry is also exemplified during the convalescent period of a coronary patient when the long period of waiting at home begins. The community wisely plans and spaces home visits that will neither tire nor completely isolate the patient.

The home visit is itself a rite of reincorporation and reentry for both the person who has lost someone by death and the person who has been divorced. These persons are often depressed and lack the initiative to "reach out" to the community. They must be "reached out to" instead.

Some of the rituals mentioned in the following pages have received serious attention by the churches; the funeral, for example, has been invested with distinct meaning for the relationship to God and to the community of faith. Other rituals, no less common, have seemingly gone unnoticed or been ignored by the churches; they have not been structured to build the relationship to God and to the Christian community. Pastors ought to notice, take seriously, and lead in the development of distinctly religious meanings for these unnoticed and ignored rituals.

The Rituals of Anticipatory Grief

Wittingly or unwittingly as a person begins to move toward death in the process of a terminal illness the pastor normally falls into step with a definable pattern of rituals that relate to the patient, the family, and the medical profession. These rituals, so far as I know, have never been "written down." Certainly there are no liturgies detailing the rites through which a family, a doctor, a hospital, and the church communicate with the dying patient. The reader will need to use his or her own imagination and empathy as we make here a first attempt to identify and describe them.

Urging

Many patients refuse to accept the fact that there is anything wrong with them. They resist going to a physician. The spouse—or the parent in the case of a child or a single adult—then enters upon a ritual of urging. If they themselves are unsuccessful in the urging, the spouse or parenting person usually invites others to join in the ritual. If there are grown sons or daughters, they are asked to speak up and use their influence. The pastor may well be one of the first persons outside the family itself to be told of the situation and asked to "urge" the person to go to a doctor for consultation. The doctor, alerted by a family member, may join indirectly in the urging. Indeed, regular annual checkups are a part of the medical profession's technique of urging. Programs for early detection of cancer in the colon, lungs, or cervix are all attempts to routinize the examination process. They program people to spread the rituals of urging over the entire life span instead of waiting for symptoms severe enough to force themselves upon the consciousness of the patient and of others as well.

Diagnosis

Sooner or later a disease produces enough symptoms to impede a patient's work or play. When this happens, life itself takes over the process of urging, and life will not temporize or take no for an answer. Then, if not before, the patient goes to a doctor or a doctor is summoned, and the rituals of diagnosis set in. One might call early diagnosis a "rite of separation" from the ranks of the well. These first attempts at diagnosis often are on an outpatient basis.

The "transitional rite" tends to be hospitalization, which is a one-word term for twenty-four hour nursing attention, observation, and charting—the rituals for which the priestesses of the hospital setting, the nurses, are trained and responsible. This ritual is usually accompanied by "some more tests," a phrase repeated almost in litany fashion by doctors, nurses, patient, and family.

Diagnosis as a "rite of reincorporation" into the community takes place when it points definitively to terminal illness. The exact orchestration of this ritual involves deciding who will be told, when, by whom, and how. The drama tends to follow one of several scripts: (1) The doctor-patient relationship is open, candid, and secure. The doctor, therefore, levels with the patient and leaves it with the patient to "put your house in order." (2) The doctor tells one or more members of the family and agrees with them as to whether the patient should be told, how much the patient should be told, and who should do the telling. (3) The patient figures things out for himself or herself, keeps up a sturdy front of denial in order to protect the family, but needs someone in whom to confide. Often the pastor, the chaplain, or a close friend is that chosen person. (4) No one tells anyone anything and a set of nonverbal games take the place of communication, leaving the patient to face death in isolation.

Gathering the Family

The next ritual, as the condition deteriorates, has members of the family coming from considerable distances to see the patient. I have known seriously ill patients to "wait," as it were, until they have seen their loved ones, personally in order to tell them "good-bye" before they die. This ritual is an extremely important one for the patient as well as for each member of the family. Intimate friends often have the same need to meet the patient "in time," both for themselves and for their dying friend.

Where the pastor has known the people involved for a long time, the unique ministry connected with the ritual is often a blend involving the confession of harbored sins and the planning of the funeral. I have known patients who were unusually matter-of-fact with me about their funeral plans. Some have even "commissioned" me to give special care to a particular loved one. The pastor can play a unique function in relation to the "gathering" of the extended family and the attendant leave-taking.

Prolonging the Inevitable

Modern medicine technology has the capacity repeatedly to resuscitate patients in cardiac arrest, through intravenous feeding to extend the life of patients who can no longer eat or drink, to extend the breathing capacity of the patient, and through the use of various machines extend the action of some organs of the body. These measures themselves constitute elaborate rituals about which debate will continue to occur: Should such measures be used at all to extend the life of a patient artificially? If so, how long?

The pastor can be the catalyst in stimulating conversation amongst the patient, the family, and attending medical personnel as to the ethical issues at stake. The family faces the dilemma on the one hand of feeling that these artificial efforts are but for the moment and futile, and on the other of not wanting to let their loved one die without having exhausted every resource for keeping him or her alive. The doctors face the dilemma of trying to draw a fine line of distinction between what is merely an extraordinary measure for actually maintaining a life and what is rather a lost cause in the sense that it substitutes medical technology for life itself. They must confront both the ethical issues and the legal definitions as to what constitutes death: Is a person dead when heart action ceases? Not necessarily; traditionally, this has been regarded as a sign of death, but technology has now brought many people to health even after their hearts have stopped. A deeper question has emerged: How long can the brain survive undamaged without an active heart supplying it with blood? This question focuses the issue of death on the brain. Increasingly, medical personnel are defining death in terms of "braindeath": the total of massive collapse of brain activity means death has really come, even though functioning of heart and lungs may be continued artificially.

Some persons have anticipated the decision their relatives may have to face and while still in good health, at the peak of their awareness, they have written detailed instructions in the form of a "living will." They direct their relatives to use no technological means to maintain their lives when all hope for meaningful existence is gone. They ask to be allowed to die peacefully, without any extraordinary prolongation of life beyond the point of no return. However, the decision is reached and announced, the discussion and determinations on this matter of prolongation involve rituals of which the pastor needs to be aware.

Notification

Death comes. The battle is over. In the hospital when a patient has died, the chaplain is routinely notified. If the family has a parish pastor, the nurses will notify him or her provided the family or the patient has requested it. A chaplain or a pastor stands with the family in this poignant time of separation and loss.

This whole matter of notification is a common and important ritual. When a soldier is killed, "notification of the next of kin" is a responsibility of the military chaplain. In the time of war, this ritual touches closely upon the anticipatory grief that the family has been experiencing—"bracing" themselves for—ever since their loved one went into basic training. In the civilian situation, where the closest kin are usually present at the time of death, the chaplain or pastor can initiate the ritual by asking if he or she can call any other relatives and friends of the family. Hospital chaplains often find that the family wants their minister, priest, or rabbi notified at once.

Funeral Planning

Sometimes the deceased has already planned the funeral in advance with the pastor. This is often true of the person who faces death knowing that there are no close relatives at hand. Psychologically speaking, a pastor is occasionally the "closest kin" some people have.

More often, it is the bereaved family that participates in the ritual of funeral planning, and this is done after the fact of death. I have, of course, had families initiate the ritual—plan the funeral—before the actual moment of death; then these matters are "taken care of before the last minute," as the young wife of a dying husband once put it when she asked for a conference on the matter.

Many factors need to be dealt with in the ritual of funeral planning. Though quickly enumerated, their importance cannot be minimized—it can rank in significance with the ritual of the funeral itself.

The place of burial must be determined. If transportation of the body from one place to a distant place is needed, this is usually done through funeral directors at the point of origin and point of destination. Air cargo is usually the preferred mode of transportation for long distances and schedule arrangements are usually made by the local funeral director in consultation with the family. It may be a matter of personal preference, but I encourage the family to avoid long distance transportation of the corpse wherever possible.

The social security number of the deceased must be located. The funeral director will need this in applying for burial benefits due the family at this time. Rarely will these benefits cover the cost of anything but a pauper funeral. They are adequate enough, however, to relieve the financial strain on most families. The pastor can mention this to the family and perhaps save them from the extra efforts that might otherwise be required to find the number. The pastor can also mention that a full set of clothing for the deceased, including socks or hose and underwear, will be requested by the funeral director.

A funeral director must be chosen. The family often asks the pastor to recommend a funeral director, particularly if this is the first time they have been through a loss by death. Otherwise older persons in the family circle—persons who have buried loved ones before—tend to have an already established relationship to a preferred funeral director.

Such families will often wish to follow also the same funeral format as before. For example, I once conducted a funeral for which the deceased's widow and I planned the service together. Sixteen years later, when the widow was dying, she simply said: "I want you to conduct my funeral. You know exactly what I want done." I replied: "I assume you want me to use the same services I used at your husband's funeral?" She answered simply: "Yes!" I knew not only the funeral director but the order of service as well.

A minister must be chosen. A pastor should always leave the choice of an officiating minister "open" and not assume anything on that score—except of course in the case of foregone conclusions like the specific prior request and instruction of the deceased that he or she be the one to officiate. Conducting the funeral ceremony is a kind of public "spotlight" ministry. Often the family will wish to choose more than one minister in order not to offend anyone. My practice is to encourage the family at a time like this to free themselves of such need to please. Also, I encourage them to use the services of (a) as few ministers as possible, preferably one, and specifically (b) the one they are most helped by and most want, (c) one who will be most accessible to them and can give them continuing attention after the funeral. Unless there is some special alienation, the parish pastor is the optimum choice. As a professor-chaplain, I usually encourage the family to rely on their "home" pastor.

Hymns, lessons, and prayers must be chosen. Some families have definite ideas about the particular hymns, Scriptures, and prayers to be used in the funeral ceremony. The pastor is sometimes prone to choose his or her own "favorites" in such planning, or to prescribe those liturgically assigned. Empathy, nonpossessive warmth, and genuineness are important criteria in making these determinations. Empathetically, the pastor gives preference to the family's frame of reference over his or her own predilections in these matters. Although the choices should be made consonant with the family's own basic belief system as far as possible, "phony" sentimentalism should be avoided.

The purpose of the ritual needs to be kept in mind by those who engage in it. Funeral planning serves certain primary functions and it is often not amiss to mention some of them to the family:

First, the funeral gives visual reality to the death. In urban, middle-class America the family and friends who are truly close to the deceased in a profound sense are usually few in number; these persons should probably *see* the body of the dead as a part of their facing reality. In rural communities and among the urban poor the boundaries of intimacy are frequently much more extended; the death of an individual affects more people. In a mountain community, for example, the clan responds as a clan, as a corporate personality, to the death of one of its members. For these reasons, a "viewing of the remains," either at the funeral home prior to the funeral or after the funeral itself at a church or funeral home, is still practiced by many people. Empathy seems to me to suggest that the decision on this point be allowed to depend on the extent of the intimate kinship at the corporate level.

Second, the funeral sets the smaller grieving family into the larger context of the extended family of the church, and even into the fellow-feeling of the larger family embracing all mankind.

Third, the funeral encourages the honest expression of grief —with its attendant feelings of loneliness, anger and injustice, frustration, relief, and celebration. All these emotions are mingled and should be recognized in prayer, music, and choice of Scripture.

Fourth, the funeral admonishes us against worship of the dead and helps us to affirm memory, life, and hope.

Fifth, the funeral celebrates the ongoingness of the contribution of the deceased to the community, and allows the community to bid the deceased farewell; to say good-bye is as important as eulogy, if not more so.

Resource books for planning a funeral are available and can be suggested. Obviously, the scriptural words of comfort are indispensable. The Psalms can give expression to any emotion a bereaved person may have. Carefully selected with a view to the family's state of mind or attitude, different sections from the Psalms will articulate in an "OK before God" way the genuine feelings of the mourners. Jesus, facing his own death on the cross, quoted Psalm 22. Romans, 1 Corinthians, and Revelation have specific and meaningful references to death and resurrection as such. Other books abound with helpful suggestions.*

Gift Bearing

The ritual of gift bearing is motivated by a desire to comfort the bereaved. The commercialized but often meaningful gift of flowers in comfort of the living and in honor of the dead is common in American culture. Many families request that instead of flowers gifts be made to various charities, not the least among which are the Cancer Fund and the Heart Fund.

A pastor may extend his or her counsel by being somewhat innovative in gifts. For example, a copy of Granger Westberg's little book *Good Grief* has been deeply appreciated by many families I know.† I overdid the matter of book giving on one occasion; Tennyson's *In Memoriam*, which had meant much *to me* when I lost my college roommate by death, meant little or nothing to a parishioner to whom I later gave it.

Instead of a book, the pastor may have in his or her possession a gift received earlier from the deceased, perhaps a particular Bible or a memento of some meaningful occasion, such as a gavel from a convention they had attended together. To present this special token as a gift *may* be meaningful, but meaning for the mourner, *not* the pastor should be the criterion of appropriateness.

Food sharing as a ritual tends to be a medium of communication between the people of a community and a family in mourning. The family does not feel like preparing food, much less eating it. Yet they are going to have visitors and overnight guests that need to be fed and housed. Comforters "bring a dish." The ritual may be a residue from the older Scotch-Irish "wake" where there were alcoholic beverages and much food and the funeral party became just that—a party. Such social get-togethers, especially for persons who have been out of touch for long periods of time, are rituals of family reunion, rituals which like all of the others are characterized by a kind of liturgically formulated terminology: "I am really glad to see you after all these years." "Yes, but I regret that it had to be on such a sad occasion as this."

Division of the Effects

The division of the effects, the tangible property of the deceased, involves a ritual in which the family as a whole participates. Occasionally, the pastor is consulted; more often he or she simply learns about it later in individual interviews, in groups, or in casual conversation. The ritual can either bring a group of relatives closer together or drive a divisive wedge further between them.

The ritual may be very informal, as in the case of persons who leave this world practically the same way they came into it—owning nothing except possibly their clothes, their watch, their ring, and a few mementos of value only to themselves. The ritual may be semiformal, as in the case where a will was written simply and in a straightforward way, probably after consultation with the people affected by its contents. Or, the ritual may be highly complicated, involving elaborate legal documents that establish such things as trusts and foundations.

Occasionally the pastor becomes involved in individual or group pastoral care and counseling of families caught up in the legal conflicts that ensue. Warring factions contest for their "just" portion of the estate. Once the estate is settled, the more structured rituals of grief are "over." Getting past this experience brings a sort of closure to the reality of the death. Even though the rituals are ended, the work of the pastor goes on.

Pastoral Follow-up

The community rituals fade out as the family members reinstitute their daily routines and the crowds of comforters "thin out." This sudden thin out, however, may well trigger an emotionally "toxic" reaction. Up until now, the family has been overwhelmed with attention and care, to the point that they find it a drain to continue responding, talking, saying thanks. Beyond this thinning out point the family may begin to suffer from undernourishment and lack of care. The strategy of the pastor is to "see to it" that a balance is maintained.

There are ways to accomplish this: (1) The pastor can visit, call, or write at regular intervals. The pastoral visit, telephone call, and letter are themselves individualized rituals. (2) The pastor may have a bereavement group, or the mourner may be a member of a support group, where "debriefing" is a normal function of the group. Here mourners may have the opportunity, perhaps for the first time, to tell their story and give vent to their feelings as they return from a bereavement situation. (3) First holidays without the deceased are particularly difficult for the bereaved. A visit, a telephone call, or a letter from the pastor or some other caring person in the congregation is exceptionally helpful on such holidays. When I was a parish pastor I used the days before Christmas and New Year's Day to visit or telephone persons who that year had lost someone either by death or by divorce.

One goal of such a ministry is to enable the person to grow in and through the loss experienced, and to arrive at a meaningful and purposeful decision to let grief run its course and do its work, and then to live again. Another goal is to enable the person to talk about the deceased in a mood free of undue depression, reticence, or bitterness and with a measure of enjoyment of the good memories and a realistic appraisal of the humanness of the deceased. In short, the pastor does not steer the mourner away from but helps him or her toward more open discussion of the deceased loved one.

The Rituals of Sudden Grief

Sudden grief, like anticipatory grief, has its rituals. Though the two sets of rituals are not identical in substance or in sequence, they do have much in common.

The first ritual of sudden grief is the notification of the next of kin. When the task falls to me as chaplain or pastor, my rule of heart is: direct, quick, clear, and unambiguous communication. At such a moment vagueness, euphemistic speech, or indirectness would be an unkindness equaled only by a slow surgical incision without anesthetic. A quick verbal incision accords better with the essence of care: "Kristin was killed in an automobile pileup on the freeway." "Your child died on the operating table." Euphemisms like "Grandpa passed away" or "Your wife went home to her Maker" are actually well-intended *un*kindness. The deceased loved one is in fact dead, not asleep, and the bereaved needs to know that, unequivocally.

An army chaplain once had the task of telling a young soldier that his father, mother, and one brother back home had been burned to death in a fire. The soldier was momentarily stunned. Then he suddenly began to scream, beat the desk and walls with his fists, and throw his body against the door with all the force he could muster. Astonished, the chaplain had the good sense and patience to wait out the hysteria and panic; he waited a full half hour until the soldier finally sat down of his own accord, exhausted. Then the chaplain quietly repeated his message and offered his services in getting the soldier back home to "attend to things." The chaplain sustained the young soldier by his pastoral presence and concern; he did not attempt to varnish over the hard reality and thereby increase suspicion and distrust.

The second ritual of the suddenly bereaved is to get the family together. Sudden deaths usually come by heart attack, stroke, accident, or suicide. The suddenness itself probably assures a scattered rather than a gathered family. More than in the case of anticipatory grief the pastor will likely have to begin placing long distance telephone calls (a budgetary item to which finance committees should give greater attention). Rapid communication is of the essence in mobilizing the life support system needed at the time of the sudden death, namely, the persons nearest to the deceased who can come together to share the grief and to comfort one another.

The third ritual of the suddenly bereaved is often that of seeing that the body is retrieved. In a swimming accident the body may be lost for hours or days, or be forever nonretrievable. Plane accidents often make recovery of the body difficult if not impossible. Persons who die suddenly of a heart attack may be far from home, even in another country; their bodies are often difficult to recover because of legal red tape. If there is suspicion of murder, an inquest may be required, even in one's own home territory. The pastor can get the facts and relay pertinent information about the procedures to the family. Members of the church with special expertise in some of the particular problems can be called upon to provide guidance and help in solving them. Such persons immediately become part of the ongoing bereavement team helping to see the mourners through what they have to go through.

These are a few of the distinctive procedures unique to the situation of sudden death. Apart from them, the other rituals of care already discussed in connection with anticipatory grief tend to be repeated as well in the situation of sudden and acute grief.

Rituals of Separation in Divorce

Our discussion of divorce in the previous chapters, where some of the rituals of separation were mentioned, need not be repeated here. The rituals of a divorce situation differ from those associated with death in being so isolated; often they are totally devoid of any formal community expression. Divorce is that form of grief for which there are no flowers sent, no church ceremonies offered, to help persons come to grips with the reality and finality of the separation. The community tends to be brought together by death, but divided—scattered

—by divorce. The dearth of community feeling and support, the deep and distressing feeling of stigma attached, and the element of deception present in the average divorce situation all conspire to strip away most rituals where the transition from marriage to the single state is conceived. Nevertheless this transition, the separation and the reuniting of people with the single population, has its subtle rituals. We must remember that a ritual is simply a certain way of doing things when one has to go through something in life. Divorce has its rituals.

When a marriage moves toward divorce, certain private rituals occur between a couple. These usually follow a certain sequence: (1) The husband and wife cease to keep track of one another, to know where the other is. If someone phones and asks, "When will your husband/wife be home?" "Can I reach him/her elsewhere?" the answer tends to be: "I don't know." (2) The couple cease to reach out for one another in time of need. Instead, they "go it alone." They "get along on their own" or they ask someone other than their own spouse to help them. (3) The husband and wife cease to touch each other, to caress each other, to want to be near each other. There may still be displays of public affection, but these tend to be staged, even exaggerated, for the sake of the audience. Behind the facade the subtle evidences of solid relationship are missing: the loving following of the other with the eyes, the nonverbal signals of recognition, the glances of agreement. (4) The husband and wife quit having sexual relations with each other; they finally quit sleeping in the same room. (5) When they formally separate, one's "moving out of the house" is a publicly observable ritual. One or the other goes to live with relatives or takes up a separate residence in a motel, hotel, or apartment, perhaps alone, perhaps with a friend or paramour.

Whereas in grief by death many of the rituals involve medical personnel, in grief by separation and divorce the rituals are related mostly to the legal profession. Again, there is a consistent sequence: (1) consultation of a lawyer to be advised of "legal rights and liabilities" (2) "filing for divorce" (3) dividing the property and deciding on parental responsibilities and access to children (4) court settlement and final decree.

Pastoral rituals are almost nonexistent in connection with this particularly painful instance of human distress. The churches *as churches* have few or no positive rites of support. Negative sanctions—at least until recently—have sometimes forbidden divorcées to participate in the Eucharist, to hold office in the church, or to be remarried with official ceremonies and blessings. Some churches permit the pastoral blessing of a civil ceremony while at the same time forbidding use of the church's own ceremony at the remarriage of a divorcée.*

Yet, individual pastors have instituted a pattern of loosely structured rituals of a less formal kind: (1) They practice bereavement counseling complete with follow-up visits, telephone calls, and letters for the divorced person as for the person who has lost someone by death. (2) They form parental guidance groups for divorcées as for parents who have lost a spouse by death. (3) They seek to develop a life support system for divorcées by getting them in touch with persons of their own sex who have suffered the same kind of separation and loss.

These rituals are usually initiated by the pastor as an official representative of the church, yet working on his own. The loneliness of the divorcée is matched by the solo efforts of the pastor, the church being only symbolically involved. The church's neglectfulness of newlyweds is matched—indeed surpassed—only by its ostracism of the divorced. One could probably defend the hypothesis that a church's ostracism of divorced persons is directly proportional to its neglect of premarital guidance for engaged couples and post-marital support of newlyweds.

Conclusion

Grief and Separation and the Life of Faith

Faith is described in the Book of Hebrews as characterizing those who do not "shrink back" from times of testing and "lose their souls." The view of the pastoral care and counseling set forth here suggests that grief and separation are such times of testing. They involve processes that we do not simply *go* through but that we *grow* through. We do not simply "put up with" such trials. We do not just stoically endure the suffering of grief and separation. On the contrary, we are people of adventure who by faith wrestle with loss of loved ones through death, divorce, or any other separating power, and the struggle goes on until fresh hope, new growth, and greater potential of life are revealed to us.

John Bunyan, in his *Pilgrim's Progress*, tells us of Christian and Pliable falling into the Slough of Despond on their way from the City of Destruction to the Celestial City.* Mr. Pliable got out first, says Bunyan, because he got out of the Slough of Despond on the side that he already knew, namely, the side nearest the City of Destruction. Christian, by faith, stayed in longer because he searched until he found the side of the Slough of Despond he did *not* already know, namely, the side nearest the Celestial City.

Harvey Cox says that we are caught between nostalgia and the terror of the future.† Fearful of what awaits us, in grief we shrink back to nostalgia—we try to make time stand still, to keep things as they were, to go back to a more secure and familiar place by a way we have always known. Grief and separation are dark times of testing. They push us into our own particular Slough of Despond.

But faith provides another alternative, and the just are saved by faith. In our sense here, faith is the commitment to grow, through events like bereavement and separation, by reliance upon a living God who is always renewing life through faith's response to the claims of growth. The "asunderness" of life is healed not by nostalgia but by translating our terror of the future into reverence for God and faith in God. I like the spirit of the prayer once handed me by a chaplain:

> Dear God,
> I have no idea where I am going. I do not see the road ahead of me. I cannot know for certain where it will end, and the fact that I think I am following your will does not mean that I am actually doing so. But I believe this: I believe the desire to please you does in fact please you. I hope I have that desire in everything I do. I hope I never do anything apart from that desire. And I know that if I do this you will lead me by the right road though I may know nothing about it at the time. Therefore, I will trust you always though I may seem to be lost, and in the shadow of death, I will not be afraid because I know you will never leave me to face my troubles alone.
>
>   Amen.

The bereaved or separated person cannot always depend upon the church, or even upon a minister. But neither can the pastor! The bereaved or separated person and the minister too both suffer some of the same kinds of grief, even if in differing ways. Both can pray, as I like to pray:

> Thank you, God
> For all you have given me
> For all you have taken from me
> For all you have left with me.

The pastor does authentic caring and counseling only out of his or her own being. As Paul says in 2 Corinthians 1:3–7, we comfort those who are in *any* affliction by means of the comfort wherewith God has comforted us. We ourselves become acquainted with grief and separation. Death and divorce do not bypass our homes, our loved ones. We pace the ramparts of eternity with our prayers as we see our sons go into service and combat—or into protest and exile. We see the work of decades collapse, as it were, before our very eyes. We see people in whom we have invested years of loyalty turn and rend us, or betray us, or simply become indifferent to us once we are of no more use to them in meeting their needs. We too face the temptations of nostalgia, cynicism, despair, and grandiose fantasies about how great we are.

Yet, in the disciplines of worship, we can bring these bruising and breaking experiences into new focus and sharper perspective. We can grow through the hurt with all the help we can draw from our community and from God. We turn then and strengthen others by sharing our own awareness of grief and by opening ourselves to new learning from them. Perhaps the clearest guidance for appreciating, counseling, and caring for the bereaved and estranged persons we meet comes in the suggestion of an East Kentucky farmer-miner. Robert Coles, a Harvard psychiatrist, has recorded the mountaineer's wisdom for ministers, and reacted to it:

> That minister should go and pray for us. He should ask God to make him a better minister, so that he'll be able to talk with us and, you know, be more a part of us—know us and not always be giving us those lessons on what *we* should do and how *we* should live. *He* should do some things, too—so *he* can be better and live better, because it's not just us that have to change our thinking, like he keeps on telling us to do. How does he know what I'm thinking? Has he ever asked me? And has he asked himself—asked himself what *he's* thinking, and if *he* should go and change anything in *his* thinking? He says he wants to help us, but he doesn't really want to see the world as we do. Maybe he should do us a favor and hear us for a change, and then go back to his side of the fence and ask himself if the people over there have anything more important to say.*

Then I felt close to that minister—and rightly warned.

Notes

Page

ix *Elisabeth Kübler-Ross, *On Death and Dying* (New York: Macmillan Co., 1969).

9. *See Frederick Perls, Ralph Hefferline, and Paul Goodman, *Gestalt Therapy: Excitement and Growth in the Human Personality* (New York: Julian Press, 1951), especially pp. ix, x, 189, 210, 211–24.

9. †"Confluence" is a state of consciousness in which a person's sense of the boundary of himself and/or herself is lost. The person cannot tell where his or her thinking and that of others begins and ends. For example, the bereaved person cannot draw a good boundary between what the deceased loved one thought and what her or she thinks.

12. *Erich Lindemann, "Symptomatology and Management of Acute Grief," *American Journal of Psychiatry* 1 (1944): 141–48.

12. †Kübler-Ross.

12. ‡See Carl Rogers, "A Theory of Therapy, Personality, and Interpersonal Relationships" in *Psychology: A Study of a Science*, ed. Sigmund Koch (New York: McGraw-Hill, 1959), p. 206. Simply put, a person is "congruent" when his own perceptions of his own feelings are clear, and he can put them into words, and his description of his feelings is accurate.

12. §Wolfgang Kohler, *Gestalt Psychology* (New York: Liveright Publishers, 1929), p. 64.

13. *Perls, Hefferline, and Goodman, pp. 146–188.

13. †Ibid., pp. 359–60.

13. ‡Ibid., p. 360.

13. §Kübler-Ross, pp. 34–159.

14. *Perls, Hefferline, and Goodman, p. 451.

18. *Muriel James and Dorothy Jongeward, *Born to Win* (New York: Addison-Wesley, 1971), pp. 217–18.

19. *Forms for these exercises can be found in Robert Neale, *The Art of Dying* (New York: Harper & Row, 1973), pp. 2, 3, 5.

19. †James and Jongeward, pp. 151–53.

20. *James Agee, *A Death in the Family* (New York: Avon Publications, 1957).

20. †Leo Tolstoy, *The Death of Ivan Illyich and Other Stories* (New York: Signet Classics, 1964).

20. ‡C. S. Lewis, *A Grief Observed* (New York: Seabury, 1963).

Page

20. §Betty Bryant, *Leaning into the Wind: The Wilderness of Widowhood* (Philadelphia: Fortress Press, 1975).

20. ||A descriptive survey of experiments. For one of the most comprehensive of this sort see Thomas E. Dougherty, "An Appraisal of Death Education in Clinical Pastoral Education" (doctoral diss., Southern Baptist Theological Seminary, Louisville, Ky., 1974).

21. *Walter B. Cannon, *The Wisdom of the Body* (New York: W. W. Norton, 1939).

22. *Wayne E. Oates, *Anxiety in Christian Experience* (Waco, Tex.: Word Books, 1972).

24. *Eric Berne, *Transactional Analysis in Psychotherapy* (New York: Grove Press, 1961), pp. 102–3.

25. *Oates, *Pastoral Counseling* (Philadelphia: Westminster Press, 1974).

26. *See Ethel Nash, Lucie Jessner, Wilfred Alse, *Marriage Counseling in Medical Practice* (Chapel Hill, N.C.: University of North Carolina Press, 1964).

30. *Guidance for the conduct of such groups is offered by Howard J. Clinebell, Jr. and Charlotte Clinebell in their book, *The Intimate Marriage* (New York: Harper & Row, 1970). The pastoral opportunities inherent in such group work are detailed in an earlier volume of this series: Howard J. Clinebell, Jr., *Growth Counseling for Marriage Enrichment: Pre-Marriage and the Early Years* (Philadelphia: Fortress Press, 1975).

31. *The local Parents Without Partners is usually listed in the telephone directory; the national office is at 1006 Via Granada, Livermore, CA 94550.

31. †Kübler-Ross, pp. 34–159.

32. *William Goode, *After Divorce* (Glencoe, Ill.: Free Press, 1956).

34. *Helpful texts include books like Ernest White, *Marriage and the Family in the Bible* (Nashville: Broadman Press, 1965); William G. Cole, *Sex and Love in the Bible* (New York: Association Press, 1961); Roland Bainton, *Sex, Love, and Marriage: A Christian Survey* (Glasgow, Scotland: William Collins, 1962).

37. *G. Thomas Shires, *Shock*, vol. 13, *Major Problems in Clinical Surgery* (Philadelphia: W. B. Saunders, 1973), p. 4.

37. †Jurgen Ruesch, *Therapeutic Communication* (New York: W. W. Norton, 1961), p. 393.

39. *Alfred Tennyson, *In Memoriam* 5, lines 5–8.

40. *Behavior modification counselors and their basic procedures are best described for the pastor in Halmuth H. Schaeffer and Patrick L. Martin, *Behavioral Therapy* (New York: McGraw Hill, 1969).

40. †See Fritz Perls, *The Gestalt Approach & Eye witness to Therapy* (Ben Lamond, Cal.: Science & Behavior Books, 1973), pp. 53, 89–90.

43. *Tennyson, *In Memoriam* 64, lines 17–20.

Page

44. *Sigmund Freud, *A General Introduction to Psychoanalysis*, trans. Joan Riviere (New York: Garden City Publishing Co., 1943), p. 166.

44. †Willard Waller and Reuben Hill, *The Family: A Dynamic Interpretation*, rev. ed. (New York: Dryden Press, 1951), pp. 476 ff.

46. *Catherine Marshall, *To Live Again* (New York: McGraw Hill, 1957).

48. *M. Proust, *Cities of the Plain* (New York: Random House, 1930), p. 238.

48. †Edna St. Vincent Millay, "Lament," lines 15–22. From *Collected Poems* (New York: Harper & Row, 1956). Copyright, 1921, 1948 by Edna St. Vincent Millay and Norma Millay Ellis. Reprinted by permission.

50. *James and Jongeward, p. 11.

52. *Kübler-Ross, p. 143.

54. *See Howard W. Stone, *Suicide and Grief* (Philadelphia: Fortress Press, 1972).

57. *These variations have been noted by such researchers as Sigmund Freud, Erich Lindemann, and others who have been mentioned in this book.

57. †"Stand Up, Stand Up for Jesus," stanza 3, lines 3–4.

58. *Andras Angyal, *Neurosis and Treatment* (New York: John Wiley & Sons, 1965), pp. 99–116.

61. *See Michael Hester, "The Use of the Telephone as a Pastoral Resource" (Master's thesis, Louisville, Ky.: Southern Baptist Theological Seminary, 1974).

61. †On the structuring of individual counseling and growth group sessions see Howard J. Clinebell, Jr., *Basic Types of Pastoral Counseling*; Wayne E. Oates, *Pastoral Counseling*; and Howard J. Clinebell, Jr., *The People Dynamic*.

62. *Arnold van Gennep, *The Rites of Passage*, trans. Monika Vizedom and Gabrielle L. Caffee (Chicago: The University of Chicago Press, 1960).

71. *See, e.g., Ernest A. Payne, Stephen F. Winward, and James W. Cox, *Minister's Worship Manual* (New York: World Publications, 1969); Charles Wallis, ed., *The Funeral Encyclopedia* (New York: Harper & Row, 1953); and Wayne E. Oates, *The Bible in Pastoral Care* (Grand Rapids: Baker Book House, 1972).

71. †Granger Westberg, *Good Grief* (Philadelphia: Fortress Press, 1962).

77. *Wayne E. Oates, *Pastoral Counseling and Social Problems*.

78. *John Bunyan, *Pilgrim's Progress* (New York: Holt, Rinehart & Winston, 1961), p. 15.

78. †Lecture delivered in Charlotte, North Carolina, March, 1973.

80. *Robert Coles, *Migrants, Sharecroppers, Mountaineers*, vol. 2, *Children of Crisis* (Boston: Little, Brown & Co., 1971), p. 617.

Annotated Bibliography

Asquith, Glenn H. *Death Is All Right.* Nashville: Abingdon, 1970. Writing in his own later years, the author sees death as an experience that need not be as negative and morbid as we make it; it is part of the normal process of life, and our thoughts about it need not be like a blight over the spirit, filled with sad images and causing us to grow sick at heart.

Bowers, Margaretta; Jackson, Edgar N.; and Knight, James A. *Counseling the Dying.* New York: Thomas A. Nelson, 1964. One of the early books on death and dying, written for ministers from an interdisciplinary point of view by a minister and two psychiatrists, it deals specifically with the counseling of dying persons.

Clinebell, Howard J., Jr. *Basic Types of Pastoral Counseling.* Nashville: Abingdon, 1974. A comprehensive survey of the field of pastoral counseling from the point of view of how it is being done, how it can be done, and what the pastor needs to know about the processes of all effective pastoral counseling, including counseling of the dying and the bereaved.

————. *The People Dynamic.* New York: Harper & Row, 1972. Provides a "growth" perspective for establishing groups which can be used effectively in connection with death education in the church, the home, the hospital for the acutely ill, and the nursing home for the chronically ill; includes a section on bereavement recovery groups plus principles for working with groups for the bereaved or for persons who are terminally ill but still ambulatory.

Feifel, Herman, ed. *The Meaning of Death.* New York: McGraw Hill, 1959. A symposium on the meaning and philosophy of death—including a good chapter by Paul Tillich—

together with explorations on an empirical basis of the meaning of death for persons of different ages.

Gardner, Richard. *The Boys and Girls Book about Divorce.* New York: Science House, 1971. Faces frankly the many grave problems and unhappy feelings of children in a divorce situation, yet it is still cheerful and positive; for ages 10 and up.

Irion, Paul. *The Funeral: Vestige or Value?* Nashville: Abingdon, 1966. Evaluates the place of the funeral in our culture and demonstrates how the funeral can contribute to recovery from loss.

Jackson, Edgar. *Understanding Grief.* Nashville: Abingdon, 1957. Offers a comprehensive understanding of what is involved in the grief process and how to deal with these dynamics in the pastoral situation.

————. *Telling a Child about Death.* New York: Meredith, 1965. An appeal for the appropriate and wise inclusion of children in the family grief process, with an emphasis upon the verbalization of their feelings.

————. *When Someone Dies.* Philadelphia: Fortress Press, 1971. A small "Pocket Counsel Book" to be placed in the hands of the grief sufferer; contributes to recovery and growth through insight.

Kübler-Ross, Elisabeth. *On Death and Dying.* New York: Macmillan, 1969. The most widely used book on the subject of ministering to the dying.

Mills, Liston O., ed. *Perspectives of Death.* Nashville: Abingdon, 1969. A superb and comprehensive symposium bringing to bear on the problems of death perspectives from the whole range of theological studies—historical, biblical, theological, ethical, and pastoral.

Neale, Robert. *The Art of Dying.* New York: Harper & Row, 1974. An up-to-date exploration of the meaning of death, with special emphasis on death by suicide; includes suggestions that the pastor can use in helping people face up to the reality of their own death.

Oates, Wayne E. *Pastoral Counseling.* Philadelphia: Westminster Press, 1974. An overview of pastoral counseling for the working pastor today.

————. *Pastoral Counseling and Social Problems: Race, Sexuality, Divorce, Extremism.* Grand Rapids, Mich.: Baker Books House, 1974. One chapter is a kind of mini-seminar on the care of the divorced person.

Switzer, David. *The Dynamics of Grief.* Nashville: Abingdon, 1970. The most thorough study of grief and its process available.

Westberg, Granger. *Good Grief.* Philadelphia: Fortress Press, 1962, 1971. A small paperback road map of the spirit for the bereaved person, the best of its kind.

Vogel, Linda Jane. *Helping a Child Understand Death.* Philadelphia: Fortress Press, 1975. Sound but simple counsel for Christian parents and teachers.